The KINGDOM of GOD

I0145671

To the Body of Christ, whose minds have been blinded before they believed,
and now Father God wants to open the scriptures to you,
so that you can live the life that God has prepared for those that love Him.

The
KINGDOM
of GOD

by
JERRY W. HOLLENBECK

BOLD TRUTH

Christian Literature & Artwork
A BOLD TRUTH Publication

Unless otherwise indicated all Scripture quotations are taken from the King James Version of The Bible.

The KINGDOM of GOD - An Agrarian Society
Copyright © 2014 Jerry W. Hollenbeck

ISBN 13: 978-0-9915751-9-0

BOLD TRUTH PUBLISHING
PO Box 742
Sapulpa, Oklahoma 74067
www.BoldTruthPublishing.com

Printed in the USA. All rights reserved under International Copyright Law. All contents and/ or cover art and design may not be reproduced in whole or in part in any form without the express written consent of the Author.

Contents

Kingdom Seekers
Research & Development classes

Featuring
The Kingdom Realities Bible Study Course

Week-10-Days-1-5
Building on the Rock:

Week-11-Days-1-5
The Faith Walk of Today:

Week-12-Days-1-5
The Whole Armour of God:

Welcome

Kingdom Seekers
Research & Development
Welcome, to the Kingdom Realities Bible Study Course.

Sometimes in order to give good understanding to what's coming up, one needs to prepare the ear to hear. I'm going to say some things that if the hearers have nothing to compare it to… they will lack understanding. Week 1 days 1-5 Born Again: Are not going to be too difficult to see and understand, but when we get to Week 3. Renewing the Mind, Week 4. Exact Knowledge, and Week 5. God's Thoughts & Ways, you're going to have to have something to compare these teachings to.

We're going to be talking about the Word of God, not the man Jesus, but who He was, before He was Jesus. When I was studying this out it took me several weeks to become comfortable with trying to separate Jesus, from the Word of God, because Jesus IS the Word of God. What helped me out a lot was *Heb. 6:1a. Therefore leaving the principles of the doctrine of Christ, let us go on unto perfection….*

Jo. 1:1-3
1. In the beginning was the Word, and the Word was with God, and the Word was God.
2. The same was in the beginning with God.
3. All things were made by him; and without him was not any thing made that was made.

So…We're talking about the Word of God, by which without Him, was not anything made that was made!! In those days He didn't have a name or gender. "It"…was God's Word. An entity if you will. Now don't expect me to explain the trinity because I can't. All I know is IT, was the Word of God. In Proverbs 9:1. IT likened Itself to the female gender. *Wisdom has builded her house...*

Prv. 7:4
Say unto wisdom, Thou art my sister; and call understanding thy kinswoman:

The Word of God is designed to produce itself. We see it in Gen.1:1-26. God said, and it was so, God said, and it was so, God said, and it was so. Over and over again. Then we also see, "And God saw that it was good." We'll talk about that in a minute. God doesn't have a road grader or chain saw. He doesn't have a cordless drill or a ½ inch wrench. He does everything He does with or by, Words only.

In Isa. 55:8-11. We see clearly, God's Word is designed to produce something. Yeah but, What? OK, how about this, exactly what IT says or describes!! Let there be light!! Let the waters be separated from the waters and the dry land appear!! What is actually going on here? (Deut. 29:29a) The secret things belong unto the LORD our God: but those things which are revealed belong unto us and to our children for ever….

The Word says in Heb. 4:12b. That the Word is….a discerner of the thoughts and intents of the heart. So when God said, Light be!! The Word, not God, but His Word went out in the universe and created the sun! The Word which was IN God, knew what God was thinking, and IT knew what God intended …..AND GOD SAW THAT IT WAS GOOD!! In other words, God saw that it was done right. Why? Because the Word knew what God wanted when He said LIGHT BE!! IT knew that the sun would not have a solid surface. IT knew that there would be nuclear fission going on all the time. IT knew that it would emit light rays, gamma rays, ultra violet rays, and it would produce solar storms. The Word knew all that and more because IT was in God at the time and when God released IT, and IT went out and produced it. What? The Sun, with all it's attributes.

So let's see it in the Word.
Isa. 55:8-11
8. For my thoughts are not your thoughts, neither are your ways my ways, saith the LORD.
9. For as the heavens are higher than the earth, so are my ways higher than your ways, and my thoughts than your thoughts.
10. For as the rain cometh down, and the snow from heaven, and returneth not thither, but watereth the earth, and maketh it bring forth and bud, that it may give seed to the sower, and bread to the eater:
11. So shall my word be that goeth forth out of my mouth: it shall not return unto me void, but it shall accomplish that which I please, and it shall prosper in the thing whereto I sent it.

How does the Word produce? Simple,
Mk. 16:20
And they went forth, and preached every where, the Lord working with them, and confirming the word with signs following.

Heb. 2:4
God also bearing them witness, both with signs and wonders, and with divers miracles, and gifts of the Holy Ghost, according to his own will?

The same Word God released in Genesis now has a name and a gender. His name is Jesus, and He now lives in YOU!! What are YOU saying about your circumstances, tests, and trials? Are you saying what the world has taught you, or what your Father God has taught you? That's why it's so important to renew your minds from the worlds thoughts and ways, to God's thoughts and ways.

Alright, hold on to your seatbelt. God, through the promises, has given us WHAT TO SAY, and a WAY TO SAY IT, that will activate what we said, and bring it to pass in our lives. Then, that fact is compounded by the fact that Jesus, came along in John 14, and said, *And whatsoever ye shall ask in my name, that will I do, that the Father may be glorified in the Son. If ye shall ask any thing in my name, I will do it.* He will do what? Whatsoever YOU said!!!!!!

The KINGDOM of GOD, "An Agrarian Society." As one might expect, The KINGDOM of GOD is different than earthly kingdoms. I won't expound on earthly kingdoms because this study is not about this natural realm we live in. We're talking about The KINGDOM of GOD…a Spiritual realm!

We…all of us, that name the Name of Christ are born-again spiritual beings. We are a species of being that never existed before.

We were in God, before the world was, but when we were born on the earth, we were born a spirit, we had a soul, and we had a body. Our spirit was of God, and our flesh was of mom and dad.

Jo. 3:6
That which is born of the flesh is flesh; and that which is born of the Spirit is spirit.

Our Heavenly Father knew us before He formed us in the womb. He knew our weaknesses and our strengths. He knew our character and personalities. More importantly, He knew we would be believers.

God set up a KINGDOM and a lifestyle for us to live by before the world was.

When we reached the age of reason, which is from age 4-8 years old, the sin nature took over, we sinned and we died spiritually like Adam and Eve did in the garden. The entire species, even Jesus Himself is a born-again type of Spiritual being that will never die again. We were born-again "in Jesus" that's the significance of the new birth, eternal life…is in Him!!

The funny thing…even somewhat awkward is the fact that there is no money or any monetary value at all in this Agrarian society. No tools, no equipment or heavy machinery, no supplies with which to build anything. NO substance at all…in The KINGDOM of GOD.

Yet the Bible says that our Faith is the substance of things hoped for, and the evidence of things not seen. But we are creative beings, created in God's image and after His likeness, but we have nothing to create with!!!

So we need to take a more serious look at how The KINGDOM is set up.

In *Mk. 4:26-32*
26. And he said, So is the kingdom of God, as if a man should cast seed into the ground;
27. And should sleep, and rise night and day, and the seed should spring and grow up, he knoweth not how.
28. For the earth bringeth forth fruit of herself; first the blade, then the ear, after that the full corn in the ear.

29. But when the fruit is brought forth, immediately he putteth in the sickle, because the harvest is come.

30. And he said, Whereunto shall we liken the kingdom of God? or with what comparison shall we compare it?

31. It is like a grain of mustard seed, which, when it is sown in the earth, is less than all the seeds that be in the earth:

32. But when it is sown, it groweth up, and becometh greater than all herbs, and shooteth out great branches; so that the fowls of the air may lodge under the shadow of it.

Okay, we sow…we wait a while…and we reap what was sown. Now listen carefully, it is very important that we know what we are to sow, and where we are to sow it. Right?

Okay,
Mk. 4:14
The sower soweth the word.

Now be very careful here. Is Jesus talking about the Word of God specifically, or is He just saying that about any word, or words?

Read the passage *Mk. 4:3-15.* I think you will agree that the Word of God, specifically, is not the only part of this teaching when we consider Jo. 14:13-14, but "words"…all words, God's and man's.

Remember
Jo. 14:14
If ye shall ask any thing in my name, I will do it.

And if you will notice, we see the hearts of men is the soil we sow into, not the ground of the earth.

So we sow words into the hearts of men, and in our own hearts.

28. For the earth bringeth forth fruit of herself; first the blade, then the ear, after that the full corn in the ear.

Well how in the world can a man's heart produce a crop? The Kingdom of God is within us.

(Re-read v. 27) *And should sleep, and rise night and day, and the seed should spring and grow up, he knoweth not how.* It is not given…for us to know! How does a seed spring up and grow in the ground? Science can tell us what happens, but science can't tell us how it happens, it's the power of God!

So we are creative beings with nothing to create with.

We need to dig a little deeper in the Word of God. Hey, right here we go!! Genesis 1:1-31 will do. We see it over and over, God said, and it was so! God said, and it was so, God said, and it was so….

What was God using?…….words!!! Words are containers. When spoken in faith they carry the "substance" of things not seen.

Heb. 11:1
Now faith is the substance of things hoped for, the evidence of things not seen.

Faith will make manifest, the things not seen. We can explain how that works. Jesus, confirms God's words, and our words when spoken in faith, with signs following.

Jesus, who is the Word of God, personified, was in God when God said, Let there be Light!! There was no substance to the Light yet, the substance was in the word… "Light." God believed that the Word in Him would produce the substance of the Word itself…Light…when He spoke the word. Sure enough, the Word that was in God, went out in space and performed the doing of what God said, and created The Sun!! How did the Word that was in God know exactly what God wanted when He said Light? Simple, Heb. 4:12.

Heb. 4:12
For the word of God is quick, and powerful, and sharper than any twoedged sword, piercing even to the dividing asunder of soul and spirit, and of the joints and marrow, and is a discerner of the thoughts and intents of the heart.

Remember now, we're talking about the Word of God, which was "in God" when He said, Let there be Light!

The Word is a discerner of the thoughts and intents of the heart. Right? The Word knew what God was thinking, and what God intended, when God said, Light! So the Word went out in space and created Light the way God intended for Light to be, and God saw the Light and said that it was good. In other words, it was done right, according to what God thought and intended.

The sun was now created. The Word knew that it would not have a solid surface, but molten plasma with nuclear fission explosions going on all the time. The Word knew that the sun would give off gamma rays, light rays, ultra violet, and some harmful rays that the earth would need to be protected from. The Word, knew all of this when God said Light.

Jo. 1:1-3
1. In the beginning was the Word, and the Word was with God, and the Word was God.
2. The same was in the beginning with God.
3. All things were made by him; and without him was not any thing made that was made.

God says words, and the Word, performs the doing of what God says.

Are you with me so far?

Now God couldn't come down and save us Himself, because God is a Spirit. You can't nail a Spirit to a tree, so God sent His Word, to do the doing of salvation. And the Word, was made flesh, and dwelt among us.

Okay, we no longer have just the Word, we now have the man Christ Jesus, who did get nailed to a tree. So now, it was the Word on salvation that saved us. The Word took upon Its self flesh, and became a man. It's the Word on healing that will heal us. It's the Word on deliverance, that will deliver us, it's the Word on prosperity, that will cause us to prosper.

It's the Word, it's the Word, IT'S THE WORD!!!

Now, the Word, has taken up residence in you when you asked Him to come into your heart and save you. He is the earnest of our inheritance.

He, Jesus…is in us the same way that He was in God… when God said, "Let there be Light!"

The Word of God walked up to the disciples one day and said, *"Whatsoever ye shall ask in my name, that will I do, that the Father may be glorified in the Son. If ye shall ask any thing in my name, I WILL DO IT!!!"*

God, bless His heart, has given us a head start, or pre-school advantage. He has given us what to say, and a way to say it that will activate what we said. He has given us words…His Words, in the form of the promises, that we can become partakers of the divine nature by calling those things that be not, as though they were.

Find a promise that covers your need, speak it, doubt not in your heart, but believe what you said shall come to pass, and you will have what you said, in faith, believing, and then Jesus will confirm your words with signs following.

The Words of God? most certainly. Our own words?….YES!! If we doubt not, but believe.

So then, we sow the Word, or we sow our own words in our own hearts, and reap the harvest of what we said, AND we will see that it was good!

It was done right because the Word is in us and He knows the thoughts and intents of our hearts.

How cool is that?

You may not be able to believe for a house or a car at first, but why don't you believe for something that you could easily get for yourself, like a pair of socks?

Then hide and watch. Just see if someone doesn't come along and give you a pair of socks. Don't tell anybody what you're doing, just do it.

The Word works. It'll work every time you put it to work, if you believe! If you have prayed, and are expecting. If you're expecting….that's Faith!!

And the substance of your words is about to be made manifest by Jesus confirming your words with signs following.

That's how the system works in the Kingdom of God. Work the system!!

(Read; Mt. 21:21-22, Mk. 11:23-24, Lk. 17:6, Jo. 14:13-14, Jo. 15:7, Jo. 16:24, 1 Jo. 5:13-15)

Jas. 1:2-8
2. My brethren, count it all joy when ye fall into divers temptations;
3. Knowing this, that the trying of your faith worketh patience.
4. But let patience have her perfect work, that ye may be perfect and entire, wanting nothing.
5. If any of you lack wisdom, let him ask of God, that giveth to all men liberally, and upbraideth not; and it shall be given him.
6. But let him ask in faith, nothing wavering. For he that wavereth is like a wave of the sea driven with the wind and tossed.
7. For let not that man think that he shall receive any thing of the Lord.
8. A double minded man is unstable in all his ways.

Jas. 1:22
But be ye doers of the word, and not hearers only, deceiving your own selves.

Heb. 6:12
That ye be not slothful, but followers of them who through faith and patience inherit the promises.

Lk. 12:32
Fear not, little flock; for it is your Father's good pleasure to give you the kingdom.

■

Week-1
Born Again

Week-1-Days-1-5
Born Again:
Day-1. Flesh is Flesh / Spirit is Spirit. Jo. 3:6
Day-2. Born not of Flesh, But of God. Jo. 1:13
Day-3. A New Creature. 2 Co. 5:17-20
Day-4. Put Off Old Man / Put on New Man. Col. 3:9-10
Day-5. Dead to Sin. Ro. 6:2

●

Day - 1
Flesh is Flesh / Spirit is Spirit.
(John 3:6)

Kingdom Seekers
WEEK 1 DAY 1
12-16-13

When a person is born of Mom and Dad, that person is born both naturally and spiritually alive before God, else the term born-again would have no significance.

We are a spirit, we have a soul, and we have a body. God is the Father of your spirit, your Dad was the father of your flesh.

Because of Adam's fall, our flesh is born with the sin nature. However, the sin nature doesn't kick in till we reach the age of reason. Once we reach the age of reason and we know right from wrong, we follow the sin nature. We can't help it, we were born that way.

Now, we need a saviour!! God, has answered that need by giving us His Son, born of a woman, but with God as His Father, He was born without the sin nature. He fulfilled the Law of Moses, took upon Himself our sin, died on the cross and redeemed us back to God, and gave us His righteousness that He established while on the earth.

My point is this, we have lost our children by sickness, still birth, abortion, crib death and many other ways. We have suffered much loss.

But God, has lost nothing. He's got 'em. He's got 'em all.

They didn't have a chance to live to do any good or evil. He will not send them into eternal punishment forever, having done no good or evil.

Ladies, if you've lost a child or aborted a child in order to get that job, or scholarship, or that man you just couldn't live without, be comforted, that child will come running into your arms on that great day crying, "Mom, I've been waiting to meet you."

It'll be… a really good day… for everyone!!

I know my writing style is awkward, that only proves that I'm not a literary person, get over it. Dyslexia, has played a tragic roll all my life, compounded by the fact that English was my worst subject in school.

2 Co. 4:4
But if our gospel be hid, it is hid to them that are lost: In whom the god of this world hath blinded the minds of them which believe not, lest the light of the glorious gospel of Christ, who is the image of God, should shine unto them.

I'm showing you this at this time in order to show you that there was a time when you were an unbeliever. Then you received Jesus as saviour and were told many times and in many ways to renew your minds. *(Eph. 4:23, Col. 3:10, Ro. 12:2, Php. 2:5, 1 Co. 2:16)*

But you haven't done it, have you? You want God to do it for you, or your Pastor to do it for you, or the Sunday School teacher to do it for you. Anybody, anybody but you, yourself. When all along, clearly, God told YOU to do it!!

If you don't do it, it's not going to get done!!!

When you were born of mom and dad, you learned how to walk and talk. Isn't it amazing what kids will say? We learned the world's language, we learned how things are done in the world. The older we got, the more we learned about the world's ways of doing things.

We have been translated into The KINGDOM of GOD. We do things differently here. We think differently here. We speak differently here. No speculating, no guessing, no surmising. We have the privilege of dealing with Exact Knowledge in The KINGDOM of GOD. Knowledge that is designed to produce itself, if spoken with intent and expectation.

When we pray, if we expect what we prayed for, it will actually happen, THAT'S FAITH!!

If we're not expecting what we prayed for to happen, Jesus is not obligated to confirm our words with signs following.

Get it? Put off the old man with his ways and deeds, put on the new man which is created in righteousness and true holiness, in God's image and after God's likeness.

Go ahead and call those things that be not as though they were. The promises are God's will for His people.

1 Jo. 5:14-15
14. And this is the confidence that we have in him, that, if we ask any thing according to his will, he heareth us:
15. And if we know that he hear us, whatsoever we ask, we know that we have the petitions that we desired of him.

You are a Spiritual being created in God's image and after His likeness. Get in line with the Word of God. Don't wait for your Pastor, or your Sunday School teacher.

Heb. 6:1a
...leaving the principles of the doctrine of Christ, let us go on unto perfection..

1 Co. 2:9-10
9. But as it is written, Eye hath not seen, nor ear heard, neither have entered into the heart of man, the things which God hath prepared for them that love him.
10. But God hath revealed them unto us by his Spirit: for the Spirit searcheth all things, yea, the deep things of God.

We don't have to wait for the great by-n-by to live this life. We can begin today,.. this day.

Jer. 10:23a
The Way of man is not in himself…

●●

Day - 2
Born not of Flesh / but of God
(John 1:13)

Kingdom Seekers
WEEK 1 DAY 2
12-17-13

Jo. 1:12-13
12. But as many as received him, to them gave he power to become the sons of God, even to them that believe on his name:
13. Which were born, not of blood, nor of the will of the flesh, nor of the will of man, but of God.

Eph. 2:12 speaks of people being aliens, strangers, having no hope, and without God in the world. That was our position before we were born again of God. When we were born of mom and dad, we were born spirit, soul, and body.

When we reached the age of reason, knowing the difference between good and evil, the sin nature took over and our spirit died and became separated from God.

That's why Jesus is called the lamb slain from the foundation of the world. God knew we would need a saviour. When we asked Jesus to save us, He entered into our hearts and we were Spiritually born again…of God. When we took our place as sons and daughters, God took His place as our Father. *(See; Gal. 4:1-7 also Ro. 8:29-31)*

We are so blessed, even beyond measure, but we're sick, broke, and we just can't seem to be able to make it.

What's wrong with this picture? The enemy has kept us blinded as to who we are in Christ!!

The Church is telling us who we are. Some are even teaching us who we are. But for many, that doesn't seem to be enough. We need to be trained.

I wish Mt. 11:12 was translated differently…the energetic take it by force.

One must purpose in their heart to find out who they are in Christ, and what privileges we have in Him. *(Read; Eph. 1:1-23)*

By the way, I use the King James Version of the Bible only. I consider all of the many translations of the Bible to be paraphrased versions of the real Bible, the KJV. They are aimed, listen now, at the carnal mind of reason so that we can understand the Bible better.

The Bible may as well still be in Hebrew and Greek because if God doesn't reveal to you what you're reading, you're not going to know anyway. Truth be known, concerning The KINGDOM of GOD, no one has ever been dragged kicking and screaming, into The KINGDOM of GOD. No one has ever casually sauntered into The KINGDOM by accident. One must press in, *...the violent take take it by force. (Read 1 Co. 2:1-16 especially verses 4, 5, 14, and 16.)*

Jesus said in
Jo. 3:3
Verily, verily, I say unto thee, Except a man be born again, he cannot see the kingdom of God.

...then in
Jo. 3:5
Verily, verily, I say unto thee, Except a man be born of water and of the Spirit, he cannot enter into the kingdom of God.

He also said in
Lk. 18:16-17
16. Suffer little children to come unto me, and forbid them not: for of such is the kingdom of God.
17. Verily I say unto you, Whosoever shall not receive the kingdom of God as a little child shall in no wise enter therein.

We must be teachable!! In a recent movie it was put this way, "It's hard to fill a cup that's already full." We can also say it this way, "it's hard to teach someone something that they think they already know." Come as a child, be teachable. *(Read Mt. 11:25-30)*

1 Pet. 1:23
Being born again, not of corruptible seed, but of incorruptible, by the word of God, which liveth and abideth for ever.

Do you realize that when you lead a person to Christ, YOU, through the power of God, have just raised a dead spirit from death, into everlasting life?

We have been restored, born again in God's image and after His likeness. ...AND GREATER WORKS THAN THESE SHALL YE DO!! Yea Lord, even so.

I don't know when we first began. The Bible says, we were in God from the beginning. Before the foundation of the world. But I do know this, Jesus had a beginning just like we did. As the Word, He always was, but as Jesus, He had a beginning, born of a woman with legal right to have dominion and rule on the earth.

In other words, in order to exercise dominion on the earth, one must be born here.

The devil was not born here. He is called the god of this world. His power has been stripped from him by Jesus, and given back to The Church. The devil is a usurper. The only power he has now is the power we give him through our words and actions. He is out to steal, kill, deceive, and destroy.

GUARD YOUR WORDS!! THEY ARE THE ONLY ACCEPTED RATE OF EXCHANGE IN THE KINGDOM OF GOD!! WE MUST LEARN TO LIVE BY OUR WORDS, ONLY!!

1 Jo. 3:9
Whosoever is born of God doth not commit sin; for his seed remaineth in him: and he cannot sin, because he is born of God.

There has been a considerable amount of trouble in the Christian community over the sin question, in case you haven't noticed?

In God's eyes, there is no sin problem on the earth today. Sin has been dealt with, period!! As we have just seen in 1 Jo. 3:9 we don't sin because we can't sin. We are born of incorruptible seed.

Not only that, but in
Heb. 10:2
For then would they not have ceased to be offered? because that the worshippers once purged should have had no more conscience of sins.

(Read Heb. 10:1-14)

The devil has successfully turned this truth around. The only people on earth who are having a problem with sin, are the Christians. The world has no conscience of sin!! The enemy has taken our eyes off the finished work of Jesus, and placed them firmly on our own behavior.

Hey, I know that 1 John 1:9 is in the Bible, but either God or John put that in there to comfort us when we do wrong.

Am I saying that 1 John 1:9 is not necessary? No, because we need it from time to time to "feel" reconciled to God after we have sinned, but God doesn't need 1 John 1:9 to "feel" good about forgiving us because God has already done something about the sin. God condemned sin in the flesh so that sin could not lord it over us and condemn us after we have been saved. Jesus said, God is love. *(Read 1 Co. 13:4-7)*

You may not realize it, but you're getting your first glimpse you have ever seen of "The Perfect Law of Liberty," that's not taught in our churches either.

They wanted to kill Paul for teaching it.

James apparently got the message.

This is an entire teaching of itself. I need to write a mini-book on the subject. I pray the Lord to open the eyes of our understanding that we may know the truth of what's been written in the Bible.

As for me, what you're getting here is just one man's interpretation. You don't have to believe a word I say.

● ● ●

Day - 3
New Creature
(II Corinthians 5:17-20)

Kingdom Seekers
WEEK 1 DAT 3
12-18-2013

2 Co. 5:17-21
*17. Therefore if any man be in Christ, **he is a new creature**: old things are passed away; behold, **all things are become new.***
*18. **And all things are of God,** who hath reconciled us to himself by Jesus Christ, and hath given to us the ministry of reconciliation;*
*19. To wit, that God was in Christ, reconciling the world unto himself, **not imputing their trespasses unto them;** and hath committed unto us the word of reconciliation.*
20. Now then we are ambassadors for Christ, as though God did beseech you by us: we pray you in Christ's stead, be ye reconciled to God.
21. For he hath made him to be sin for us, who knew no sin; that we might be made the righteousness of God in him.

Let's consider...
#1. A New Creature.

We were reborn a new creature that never existed before. We were not born again out in the world on our own, we were born again "In Christ," He in us and us in Him, we were born Spiritually in God.

Those babies and young children I mentioned earlier, they are in God, but they weren't born again like we are.

NOTE: The authority and rulership that the devil tried to take from God, God created an entire race of people and gave us that authority and rulership.

Before you get upset, let me qualify that statement. In studying The KINGDOM, you find out a lot of neat stuff.

Heaven, is not promised to us in the Bible!! The Bible says, the people in heaven are waiting to come back to the earth with Jesus. When we die, we go to heaven to be with the Lord, and wait for the millenial reign of Christ, and we will return to the earth with Him.

Listen, on earth we are Kings and Queens. In Heaven, we are princes and princesses. Heaven is Father God's domain. The earth was created and given to man, so that man could have a taste of rulership. God has dominion in Heaven, we have dominion on the earth.

I don't know this but I suspect that the entire universe will end up as dominion for man. A great big sandbox for the children of the Most High God, to play in forever.

#2. All things are become new.

Here is a clear indication that we need to renew our minds from the world's way of thinking and doing things, because in The KINGDOM of GOD we think and do things differently.

Because of the promises, like God, we can see the end from the beginning of our circumstances, tests, and trials. We have the God given authority to call those things that be not as though they were and expect what we say shall come to pass.

Remember, the Word, Jesus, is now in you and He is a discerner of the thoughts and intents of the heart. HE KNOWS if you're believing for what you just said will happen or not. HE KNOWS if you're expecting or not. And you can't fool Him. If you're expecting what you said will happen, THAT'S FAITH!!

If you're not, Jesus is not obligated to confirm your words with signs following. It's as simple as that.

Don't be stupid. In The KINGDOM of GOD, we live by our words....only. No money, no silver, no gold or shinny stones. It's words only! ...in The KINGDOM of GOD.

#3. And all things are of God.

Okay, this one covers more information than one page will allow. Let's just say that we have rights and privileges, blessings and promises that we didn't have before.

#4. Not imputing their trespasses unto them.

Here's another glimpse of the Perfect Law of Liberty. The Perfect Law of Liberty is new revelation to me, fresh manna from Heaven, it's not in this Bible study course yet, but it will be. I know you're curious about it.

Preachers won't like it. They wanted to kill Paul because of that teaching. It will turn your world upside down and set you free!! Yes, set you free from the self condemnation trips and the frustration of the sin which is still in your life.

God has done something about it. All of it!! Relax, we should have no conscience of sin. And you won't when you see and understand The Perfect Law of Liberty.

I know I use a lot of commas, and dot, dot, dots. I only do it to break up a sentence, emphasize a point, or state a conclusion. I never clamed to be an author, writer, or literary person. Bear with me, we'll get through this.

Mt. 18:3-4
3. Verily I say unto you, Except ye be converted, and become as little children, ye shall not enter into the kingdom of heaven.
4. Whosoever therefore shall humble himself as this little child, the same is greatest in the kingdom of heaven.

Mt. 23:11
But he that is greatest among you shall be your servant.

Lk. 22:23-26
23. And they began to inquire among themselves, which of them it was that should do this thing.
24. And there was also a strife among them, which of them should be accounted the greatest.
25. And he said unto them, The kings of the Gentiles exercise lordship over them; and they that exercise authority upon them are called benefactors.
26. But ye shall not be so: but he that is greatest among you, let him be as the younger; and he that is chief, as he that doth serve.

In an earthly kingdom, the king is supported by his subjects by way of taxes, tributes, and such.

Did you notice that in GOD'S KINGDOM, God provides, protects, blesses, delivers, and takes care of the people? In GOD'S KINGDOM, we don't have authority over each other. We are all given a free will.

However, we do have authority over another person's body. Why? Because their body is made of the earth. We have dominion over the earth. Every thing in it, on it, and above it.

Jesus came in a servant's capacity. The greatest among us will be our servants. The one you are ministering to may not have the faith to be healed, but you do!! Do as you were instructed, lay hands on him, pray the prayer of faith over him, give him a prayer cloth, or spit on him if God tells you to.

From the ridiculous to the logical, we are a peculiar people predestinated to show forth the manifold wisdom of God.

Jo. 14:12-14
12. Verily, verily, I say unto you, He that believeth on me, the works that I do shall he do also; and greater works than these shall he do; because I go unto my Father.
13. And whatsoever ye shall ask in my name, that will I do, that the Father may be glorified in the Son.
14. If ye shall ask any thing in my name, I will do it.

Jo. 15:16
Ye have not chosen me, but I have chosen you, and ordained you, that ye should go and bring forth fruit, and that your fruit should remain: that whatsoever ye shall ask of the Father in my name, he may give it you.

We are fearfully and wonderfully made, the crowning glory of God's creation. *(Read: Psa. 139)* It's about you!! I encourage you to renew your mind to who you are in Christ.

●●●●

Day - 4
Put off the old man / Put on the new man.
(Colossians 3:9-10)

Kingdom Seekers
WEEK 1 DAY 4
12-19-2013

The main thrust of Kingdom Seekers is to help new and old Christians change the way they think, the way they talk, and the way they live on the earth.

2 Pet. 1:11
For so an entrance shall be ministered unto you abundantly into the everlasting kingdom of our Lord and Saviour Jesus Christ.

Lk. 12:32
Fear not, little flock; for it is your Father's good pleasure to give you the kingdom.

Putting off the old man is not going to happen over night.

It's going to be a process because,
Ro. 5:8
But God commendeth his love toward us, in that, while we were yet sinners, Christ died for us.

Honestly, it's only been 4 days since I started this teaching and the Lord has been flooding me with new revelations. I've been waiting for God to open doors for me but it appears that God was waiting for me to set about the Father's business.

Now that I have done it, WOW, a fresh wind of revelation has come!! *(Read Gal. 3:1-29)*

This will be a great revelation for new believers and answer a very big question for older Christians.

Pay close attention to these verses *Gal. 3:6-14.*
6. Even as Abraham believed God, and it was accounted to him for righteousness.
7. Know ye therefore that they which are of faith, the same are the children of Abraham.
8. And the scripture, foreseeing that God would justify the heathen through faith, preached before the gospel unto Abraham, saying, In thee shall all nations be blessed.
9. So then they which be of faith are blessed with faithful Abraham.
10. For as many as are of the works of the law are under the curse: for it is written, Cursed is every one that continueth not in all things which are written in the book of the law to do them.
11. But that no man is justified by the law in the sight of God, it is evident: for, The just shall live by faith.
12. And the law is not of faith: but, The man that doeth them shall live in them.
13. Christ hath redeemed us from the curse of the law, being made a curse for us: for it is written, Cursed is every one that hangeth on a tree:
14. That the blessing of Abraham might come on the Gentiles through Jesus Christ; that we might receive the promise of the Spirit through faith.

Did you notice that The Gospel was preached to Abraham? He believed God, that one was coming that would save God's people from their sin. IT WAS ACCOUNTED TO HIM FOR RIGHTEOUSNESS!!! That's important, those of us who also believe, should be blessed like faithful Abraham. Right?

Now look at verse 10. *Those that are of the works of the law are under the curse.*

NOT THOSE THAT ARE UNDER THE LAW, UNBELIEVERS, BUT THOSE THAT ARE OF THE WORKS OF THE LAW!! BELIEVERS THAT HAVE LEFT THEIR FAITH IN JESUS, AND HAVE GONE BACK TO DOING THE WORKS OF THE LAW. TOUCH NOT, TASTE NOT, HANDLE NOT.

Salvation does not consist of BELIEVE IN JESUS, AND…. IT'S BELIEVE IN JESUS PERIOD!! WITHOUT THE WORKS OF THE LAW!!

Remember the account of the woman whose husband died? Though she was married, her husband died, and she is now free to marry again without committing adultery.

Jesus took upon Himself our sin, died, and is alive again. We are born again "in Him," WE ARE DEAD TO SIN, AND ARE ALIVE AGAIN. WHERE THERE IS NO LAW, THERE IS NO TRANSGRESSION. We are not under the law, but when we try to do the works of the law, we without realizing it, put ourselves back under the curse of the law.

STOP IT!!

PUT YOUR FAITH IN WHAT JESUS DID AND STOP TRYING TO BEHAVE YOURSELF. THE PERFECT LAW OF LIBERTY.

Remember Romans 7:17 When we sin, it's no longer we that do it, but sin that dwells in us. While we were yet sinners, He died for us.

Have you ever wondered why you are still subject to sickness and money problems? What is the curse of the law? Poverty, sickness, and death.

Read the whole book of Galatians, it's all about falling from grace and going back to the law.

Gal. 3:1-5
1. O foolish Galatians, who hath bewitched you, that ye should not obey the truth, before whose eyes Jesus Christ hath been evidently set forth, crucified among you?
2. This only would I learn of you, Received ye the Spirit by the works of the law, or by the hearing of faith?
3. Are ye so foolish? having begun in the Spirit, are ye now made perfect by the flesh?
4. Have ye suffered so many things in vain? if it be yet in vain.
5. He therefore that ministereth to you the Spirit, and worketh miracles among you, doeth he it by the works of the law, or by the hearing of faith?

Gal. 3:10-12
10. For as many as are of the works of the law are under the curse: for it is written, Cursed is every one that continueth not in all things which are written in the book of the law to do them.
11. But that no man is justified by the law in the sight of God, it is evident: for, The just shall live by faith.
12. And the law is not of faith: but, The man that doeth them shall live in them.

Ro. 14:22-23
22. Hast thou faith? have it to thyself before God. Happy is he that condemneth not himself in

that thing which he alloweth.

23. And he that doubteth is damned if he eat, because he eateth not of faith: for whatsoever is not of faith is sin.

2 Pet. 3:15-16
15. And account that the longsuffering of our Lord is salvation; even as our beloved brother Paul also according to the wisdom given unto him hath written unto you;
16. As also in all his epistles, speaking in them of these things; in which are some things hard to be understood, which they that are unlearned and unstable wrest, as they do also the other scriptures, unto their own destruction.

We suffer and feel guilty because we know we're doing wrong, as if we are still yet sinners. That's why it is so, so... so important to take our eyes off ourselves and put them on Jesus and what He did. Not having our own righteousness, but the righteousness which is of God!! Perfect, without spot or blemish, or any such thing. It's not about us, it's about Jesus.

Gen. 13:1-2
1. And Abram went up out of Egypt, he, and his wife, and all that he had, and Lot with him, into the south.
2. And Abram was very rich in cattle, in silver, and in gold.

Egypt is a type of the world. We are called out of the world and translated into The KINGDOM of GOD. Abraham was very rich. In spiritual things? No!! In natural things, cattle, silver, and gold.

Our prosperity is out there waiting for us and just as soon as we leave off the works of the law and get in Faith in Jesus' finished work, WE WILL HAVE THE BLESSINGS OF ABRAHAM AND PROSPER!

3 Jo. 2
Beloved, I wish above all things that thou mayest prosper and be in health, even as thy soul prospereth.

There are many ways to teach this lesson, but for today, this is what the Lord put on my heart. We have seen Faith, the works of the law, and the perfect law of liberty.

It is no longer you that doeth it, but sin that dwelleth in you! Get over it!! Continue to grow in the knowledge of Christ.

Now I ask you, what are you going to do with this information? Stay sick and broke, or get in Faith?

● ● ● ● ●

Day - 5
"Dead to sin"
(Romans 6:2)

Kingdom Seekers
WEEK 1 DAY 5
12-20-2013

Ro. 6:2-7

2. God forbid. How shall we, that are dead to sin, live any longer therein?

3. Know ye not, that so many of us as were baptized into Jesus Christ were baptized into his death?

4. Therefore we are buried with him by baptism into death: that like as Christ was raised up from the dead by the glory of the Father, even so we also should walk in newness of life.

5. For if we have been planted together in the likeness of his death, we shall be also in the likeness of his resurrection:

6. Knowing this, that our old man is crucified with him, that the body of sin might be destroyed, that henceforth we should not serve sin.

7. For he that is dead is freed from sin.

In my actual meetings I copy my notes and hand them out. The meetings are usually 2 hours long, and the handouts are 2 full pages long, all scripture, no personal comments.

We have the privilege of dealing with "Exact Knowledge" which is coming up in Week 4-1-5. God's knowledge. God's truth. Knowledge that is so exact, so accurate, so focused, it qualifies to be a Truth. Knowledge that is so true, so exact and accurate, it qualifies to be a Law!! We'll get into that later in Week 4. I just wanted to comfort you in the fact that God's knowledge stands forever. It will not change to fit circumstances, and there is not even a shadow of turning with God's knowledge.

WE ARE DEAD TO SIN!! IT IS NOT A SIDE EFFECT, IT IS GOD'S PLAN!!

He did everything for us and as we saw yesterday, when we try to justify our behavior ourselves, we negate what Jesus did for us and try to justify ourselves by our own works. We have fallen from grace and inadvertently placed ourselves back under the curse of the law.

We punish ourselves over something we didn't even do. We don't sin, we can't sin because we are born of God. Where no law is, there is no transgression. We are dead to sin because we are in Jesus. He fulfilled the law of Moses, took upon Himself our sin, died to pay the wages for OUR sin, gave us His righteousness and now we are alive in Him.

Remember, when we try to justify ourselves by our behavior before God, we put ourselves back under the curse of the law that we have been redeemed from by Jesus.

The devil didn't do it, God didn't do it, YOU did it. That's why you're sick, "which you've been redeemed from," and that's why you're broke, "which you've been redeemed from." STOP trying to justify yourself before God. Jesus already did that.

Mt. 11:28-30
28. Come unto me, all ye that labour and are heavy laden, and I will give you rest.
29. Take my yoke upon you, and learn of me; for I am meek and lowly in heart: and ye shall find rest unto your souls.
30. For my yoke is easy, and my burden is light.

Stop carrying the burden of sin in your life, learn of Jesus and what He did for you. His yoke is easy and His burden is light and He will give you rest. What rest? The knowledge that He has taken care of everything.

Ro. 7:14-25
14. For we know that the law is spiritual: but I am carnal, sold under sin.
15. For that which I do I allow not: for what I would, that do I not; but what I hate, that do I.
16. If then I do that which I would not, I consent unto the law that it is good.
17. Now then it is no more I that do it, but sin that dwelleth in me.
18. For I know that in me (that is, in my flesh,) dwelleth no good thing: for to will is present with me; but how to perform that which is good I find not.
19. For the good that I would I do not: but the evil which I would not, that I do.
20. Now if I do that I would not, it is no more I that do it, but sin that dwelleth in me.
21. I find then a law, that, when I would do good, evil is present with me.
22. For I delight in the law of God after the inward man:
23. But I see another law in my members, warring against the law of my mind, and bringing me into captivity to the law of sin which is in my members.
24. O wretched man that I am! who shall deliver me from the body of this death?
25. I thank God through Jesus Christ our Lord. So then with the mind I myself serve the law of God; but with the flesh the law of sin.

1 Pet. 5:6-11
6. Humble yourselves therefore under the mighty hand of God, that he may exalt you in due time:
7. Casting all your care upon him; for he careth for you.
8. Be sober, be vigilant; because your adversary the devil, as a roaring lion, walketh about, seeking whom he may devour:
9. Whom resist stedfast in the faith, knowing that the same afflictions are accomplished in your brethren that are in the world.
10. But the God of all grace, who hath called us unto his eternal glory by Christ Jesus, after that ye have suffered a while, make you perfect, stablish, strengthen, settle you.

11. To him be glory and dominion for ever and ever. Amen.

Gal. 4:1-7
1. Now I say, That the heir, as long as he is a child, differeth nothing from a servant, though he be lord of all;
2. But is under tutors and governors until the time appointed of the father.
3. Even so we, when we were children, were in bondage under the elements of the world:
4. But when the fullness of the time was come, God sent forth his Son, made of a woman, made under the law,
5. To redeem them that were under the law, that we might receive the adoption of sons.
6. And because ye are sons, God hath sent forth the Spirit of his Son into your hearts, crying, Abba, Father.
7. Wherefore thou art no more a servant, but a son; and if a son, then an heir of God through Christ.

(v.3) While we were still children learning who we are in Christ, we were subject to the elements of the world.

Watch your words, they will dictate the course of your path in this world. You can live in the blessings of Abraham, or you can "do it your way" and live under the curse of the law by trying to do the "works of the law" in order to justify yourself to God for your behavior, negating what Christ has done for you.

Gal. 5:4
Christ is become of no effect unto you, whosoever of you are justified by the law; ye are fallen from grace.

Can a person be born again, again?

According to...
Gal. 4:19
My little children, of whom I travail in birth again until Christ be formed in you.

Read all of Galatians, it deals with people who were "taught" back into doing the works of the law.

When you do wrong, just thank God for Jesus, Who by His blood has saved you. He did everything, all we need do is believe and rest in the truth of it.

■ ◻

Week-2
The Righteousness of God

Week-2-Days-1-5
The Righteousness of God:
Day-1. The Mind of Christ. 1 Co.2:16, Php. 2:5-6
Day-2. Righteousness Speaks. Ro. 10:6-10
Day-3. The Disciple and The Servant. Mt. 10:24-25
Day-4. Sharper Than Any Two Edged Sword. Heb. 4:12
Day-5. The Weapons of Our Warfare. 2 Co. 10:4-5

•

Day - 1
"The Mind of Christ"
(I Corinthians 2:16, Philippians 2:5-6)

Kingdom Seekers
WEEK 2 DAY 1
12-23-2013

We can all take comfort in the fact that the righteousness that Jesus established while on the earth, is the righteousness of God. But the righteousness of God, covers so much more than that. There are things that accompany righteousness, such as the new creation. We didn't get a new body or a new spirit. But a born again "New Classification" we are born again "In Christ."

However, when we were born of mom and dad we were born a tri-part being, spirit, soul, and body. When we reached the age of reason, knowing right from wrong, good and evil, the sin nature kicked in, we sinned, and our spirits died before God.

Now we need a saviour.

When is the age of reason?

I suppose it is from 4 to 8 years old.

When you were born of mom and dad, you were born with a mind, right? It was empty, but you had one, right?

Well, when you were born of God, you were born with a mind. The mind of the spirit, which is able to discern Spiritual things.

Father God has told us to renew our minds but many of us haven't done it. So in other words, okay, son if you want to do it "your way," you're on your own, knock yourself out. You are saved but without "all" of God's influence in the world. (Read *1 Co. 2:1-16*...also; *Ro. 8:1-10. v. 6-8* in particular)

Ro. 8:6-8
6. For to be carnally minded is death; but to be spiritually minded is life and peace.
7. Because the carnal mind is enmity against God: for it is not subject to the law of God, neither indeed can be.
8. So then they that are in the flesh cannot please God.

The soul is where both minds are located. You've heard the phrase, it's all in your head, well that's right. The mind of reason and the mind of the spirit share the same space.

But wait, that's not all. We have God's promises which are designed to answer all our needs. Peter says, we have some exceeding great and precious promises. What do you suppose these could be?

How about these to name a few.

Mt. 17:20
And Jesus said unto them, Because of your unbelief: for verily I say unto you, If ye have faith as a grain of mustard seed, ye shall say unto this mountain, Remove hence to yonder place; and it shall remove; and nothing shall be impossible unto you.

Mt. 18:19-20
19. Again I say unto you, That if two of you shall agree on earth as touching any thing that they shall ask, it shall be done for them of my Father which is in heaven.
20. For where two or three are gathered together in my name, there am I in the midst of them.

Mt. 21:21-22
21. Jesus answered and said unto them, Verily I say unto you, If ye have faith, and doubt not, ye shall not only do this which is done to the fig tree, but also if ye shall say unto this mountain, Be thou removed, and be thou cast into the sea; it shall be done.
22. And all things, whatsoever ye shall ask in prayer, believing, ye shall receive.

Mk. 11:22-24
22. And Jesus answering saith unto them, Have faith in God.
23. For verily I say unto you, That whosoever shall say unto this mountain, Be thou removed, and be thou cast into the sea; and shall not doubt in his heart, but shall believe that those things which he saith shall come to pass; he shall have whatsoever he saith.

24. *Therefore I say unto you, What things soever ye desire, when ye pray, believe that ye receive them, and ye shall have them.*

Lk. 17:6
And the Lord said, If ye had faith as a grain of mustard seed, ye might say unto this sycamine tree, Be thou plucked up by the root, and be thou planted in the sea; and it should obey you.

Jo. 14:12-14
12. Verily, verily, I say unto you, He that believeth on me, the works that I do shall he do also; and greater works than these shall he do; because I go unto my Father.
13. And whatsoever ye shall ask in my name, that will I do, that the Father may be glorified in the Son.
14. If ye shall ask any thing in my name, I will do it.

Jo. 8:31-32
31. Then said Jesus to those Jews which believed on him, If ye continue in my word, then are ye my disciples indeed;
32. And ye shall know the truth, and the truth shall make you free.

Jo. 15:7
If ye abide in me, and my words abide in you, ye shall ask what ye will, and it shall be done unto you.

1 Jo. 5:13-15
13. These things have I written unto you that believe on the name of the Son of God; that ye may know that ye have eternal life, and that ye may believe on the name of the Son of God.
14. And this is the confidence that we have in him, that, if we ask any thing according to his will, he heareth us:
15. And if we know that he hear us, whatsoever we ask, we know that we have the petitions that we desired of him.

In this Bible study God is encouraging us to grow up in the knowledge of Him. We are created in righteousness and true holiness and we can grow in knowledge into the image of Him that created us, unto the stature of the fullness of Christ, on the earth, in this lifetime.

When we were born again, we were ruled by our mind of reason. As we grow in the knowledge of God, we should learn to rule through the mind of the spirit, casting down imaginations and every high thing that exalts itself against the knowledge of God, bringing into captivity every thought to the obedience of Christ.

Instead of saying what the world says about our circumstances, what's the use, we just can't make it… why don't we say what God has taught us to say? I can do all things through Christ who strengthens me, and nothing shall be impossible unto me. We have a choice, we can say what the world says, or we can say what God says.

2 Tim. 2:15
Study to show thyself approved unto God, a workman that needeth not to be ashamed, rightly dividing the word of truth.

God is not going to renew your mind. (We'll get to that next week.) He told you to do it!!! If you don't do it, it won't get done and you will live out your life on the earth as one who does not know God. Yes, you are saved, but you are without God's help in the world through His Word.

You are now living in this world according to the sum of your words. If you don't like the way life is treating you....change your words!! Say what God says about you, not what the world says about you.

●●

Day - 2
"Righteousness Speaks"
(Romans 10:6-10)

Kingdom Seekers
WEEK 2 DAY 2
12-24-2013

Ro. 10:1-10
1. Brethren, my heart's desire and prayer to God for Israel is, that they might be saved.
2. For I bear them record that they have a zeal of God, but not according to knowledge.
3. For they being ignorant of God's righteousness, and going about to establish their own righteousness, have not submitted themselves unto the righteousness of God.
4. For Christ is the end of the law for righteousness to every one that believeth.
5. For Moses describeth the righteousness which is of the law, That the man which doeth those things shall live by them.
6. But the righteousness which is of faith speaketh on this wise, Say not in thine heart, Who shall ascend into heaven? (that is, to bring Christ down from above:)
7. Or, Who shall descend into the deep? (that is, to bring up Christ again from the dead.)
8. But what saith it? The word is nigh thee, even in thy mouth, and in thy heart: that is, the word of faith, which we preach;
9. That if thou shalt confess with thy mouth the Lord Jesus, and shalt believe in thine heart that God hath raised him from the dead, thou shalt be saved.
10. For with the heart man believeth unto righteousness; and with the mouth confession is made unto salvation.

Verses 6-8.
6. But the righteousness which is of faith speaketh on this wise, Say not in thine heart, Who

shall ascend into heaven? (that is, to bring Christ down from above:)

7. Or, Who shall descend into the deep? (that is, to bring up Christ again from the dead.)

8. But what saith it? The word is nigh thee, even in thy mouth, and in thy heart: that is, the word of faith, which we preach;

We will get a much clearer picture of verses, 6 and 7 in Week-2-Day-3. The Disciple and The Servant.

But for now, let's just say that we don't need to call Jesus in person to come on the scene, we have Him in His primary identity. He is The Word of God, therefore, verse 8 and 10 come into play.

The Word in written form will produce nothing. Now please don't take offence to that statement and close your minds to what we're about to say here. In written form, the Word has the inherent power to produce what words say or describe, but written words are not "activated" to produce. Written words are like sticks of dynamite. They have the power to move mountains, but without a fuse or blasting cap, they just lay there inactive. It's only when we speak the Word, that the Word becomes activated, and will produce what was said.

Then, verse 10 comes into play.
For with the heart man believeth unto righteousness; and with the mouth confession is made unto salvation.

The word salvation, is the Greek word, "soteria." *(so-tay-ree-ah)* it means, rescue or safety, deliver, health, salvation, save, and saving.

So what's my point?

When trouble comes, find a promise that covers your need, speak it, doubt not in your heart, but believe that what you said, shall come to pass. Jesus said, if anybody would do that, they would have what they said!!

He also said, in
Mk. 4:24
And he said unto them, Take heed what ye hear: with what measure ye mete, it shall be measured to you: and unto you that hear shall more be given.

Let's pay close attention to, "with what measure ye mete, it shall be measured to you:"

Righteousness Speaks! So when you speak Righteousness things, how do you intend your words to be manifested? Do you mean to effect a rescue, or a healing? Do you mean to be delivered, or create a safety zone in a hazardous situation?

How do you mean for your words to be manifested?

I say that because the same Word that God released in the creation and restoration in Genesis, now lives in you. He is the Word, and is a discerner of the thoughts and intents of the heart. He's in you. He knows what you're thinking, and what you intend when you speak, so focus your words to express exactly what you want when you speak!!

When God said, light be!! The Word, went out and created the sun. When God said, Let the waters be separated from the waters and the dry land appear, the Word, produced the dry land.

God didn't have to lift a finger. He placed the power to produce what He says, IN THE WORDS, THEMSELVES!!

Then, in the 14th chapter of John, Jesus comes along and says,
12. Verily, verily, I say unto you, He that believeth on me, the works that I do shall he do also; and greater works than these shall he do; because I go unto my Father.
13. And whatsoever ye shall ask in my name, that will I do, that the Father may be glorified in the Son.
14. If ye shall ask any thing in my name, I will do it.

How does Jesus do it? How exactly does He produce what we say?

Mk. 16:20
And they went forth, and preached every where, the Lord working with them, and confirming the word with signs following. Amen.

Heb. 2:4
God also bearing them witness, both with signs and wonders, and with divers miracles, and gifts of the Holy Ghost, according to his own will?

These are some of the rights and privileges that accompany righteousness.

In a King's court, one does not speak unless the King acknowledges him. It used to be that a man could lose his head for speaking out unannounced in a King's court.

The Scepter of Righteousness, is the scepter of GOD'S KINGDOM. When you were born again, the Scepter of Righteousness was extended toward you, YOU MAY NOW SPEAK, and plead your case before Father God and overcome your circumstances, coming boldly into the Throne room and obtain help in time of need.

I am straining at the bit with anticipation until we get to Weeks 3, 4, 5 & 6. Together we are going to learn how to reign in life with Christ.

We don't know how to rule in this country. We don't know that much about royalty. I joke in my meetings, if you put a gun in the hand of a man in a convenience store, or a bank lobby, we will learn Rulership. Other than that, we don't know that much about Rulership in America.

Our Rulership does not extend to other people. God has given all of us a free will. We have Rulership over the earth, everything in it, on it, and over it. We cannot rule over each other, but we can exercise authority over another person's body because their body is made of the earth.

We can drive out sickness and disease out of that body in the name of Jesus, because the other person may not have the faith to do it themselves.

Have you ever noticed that Jesus never said, I take authority over this sickness or situation? He simply exercised the authority He knew He already had.

WE HAVE THAT KIND OF AUTHORITY ON THE EARTH!!

Jo. 14:12
Verily, verily, I say unto you, He that believeth on me, the works that I do shall he do also; and greater works than these shall he do; because I go unto my Father.

Jo. 15:16
Ye have not chosen me, but I have chosen you, and ordained you, that ye should go and bring forth fruit, and that your fruit should remain: that whatsoever ye shall ask of the Father in my name, he may give it you.

Heb. 6:4-6
4. For it is impossible for those who were once enlightened, and have tasted of the heavenly gift, and were made partakers of the Holy Ghost,
5. And have tasted the good word of God, and the powers of the world to come,
6. If they shall fall away, to renew them again unto....

● ● ●

Day - 3
"The Disciple and The Servant"
(Matthew 10:24-25)

Kingdom Seekers
WEEK 2 DAY 3
12-25-2013

Merry Christmas everyone.
Mt. 10:24-25
24. The disciple is not above his master, nor the servant above his lord.

25. It is enough for the disciple that he be as his master, and the servant as his lord.

Lk. 6:40
The disciple is not above his master: but every one that is perfect shall be as his master.

The word "perfect" could also be translated: thoroughly equipped, or a mature person shall be as his master.

Do you remember Paul's thorn in the flesh?

2 Co. 12:7-9
7. And lest I should be exalted above measure through the abundance of the revelations, there was given to me a thorn in the flesh, the messenger of Satan to buffet me, lest I should be exalted above measure.
8. For this thing I besought the Lord thrice, that it might depart from me.
9. And he said unto me, My grace is sufficient for thee: for my strength is made perfect in weakness. Most gladly therefore will I rather glory in my infirmities, that the power of Christ may rest upon me.

God answered him, My grace is sufficient for thee, for My strength is made perfect in weakness. God's grace, WE HAVE HIS NAME, HIS WORD, AND HIS SPIRIT!! His strength, THE POWER IS "IN" HIS WORD. In our weakness, WE CAN'T DO ANYTHING ABOUT OUR TESTS, TRIALS, AND CIRCUMSTANCES, BUT WE "CAN" SPEAK WORDS OF FAITH, ...RIGHTEOUSNESS SPEAKS!!

Gal. 4:1-3
1. Now I say, That the heir, as long as he is a child, differeth nothing from a servant, though he be lord of all;
2. But is under tutors and governors until the time appointed of the father.
3. Even so we, when we were children, were in bondage under the elements of the world:...

When we are children, we are still subject to the elements of the world, but when we grow up in the knowledge of The KINGDOM, we are under authority, and should be able to cast down all circumstances, tests, and trials with our words.

Remember the Centurion?

Mt. 8:5-10
5. And when Jesus was entered into Capernaum, there came unto him a centurion, beseeching him,
6. And saying, Lord, my servant lieth at home sick of the palsy, grievously tormented.
7. And Jesus saith unto him, I WILL COME AND HEAL HIM.
8. The centurion answered and said, Lord, I am not worthy that thou shouldest come under my roof: BUT SPEAK THE WORD ONLY, and my servant shall be healed.

9. *For I AM A MAN UNDER AUTHORITY, having soldiers under me: and I say to this man, GO AND HE GOETH; and to another, COME AND HE COMETH; and to my servant, DO THIS AND HE DOETH IT.*

10. *When Jesus heard it, he MARVELLED, and said to them that followed, Verily I say unto you, I have not found SO GREAT FAITH, no, not in Israel.*

Okay, now check out
Mt. 8:11-13

11. *And I say unto you, That many shall come from the east and west, and shall sit down with Abraham, and Isaac, and Jacob, in the kingdom of heaven.*

12. *But the children of the kingdom shall be cast out into outer darkness: there shall be weeping and gnashing of teeth.*

13. *And Jesus said unto the centurion, Go thy way; and AS THOU HAST BELIEVED, SO BE IT DONE UNTO THEE. And his servant was healed in the selfsame hour.*

Heb. 12:1-3

1. *Wherefore seeing we also are compassed about with so great a cloud of witnesses, let us lay aside every weight, and the sin which doth so easily beset us, and let us run with patience the race that is set before us,*

2. *Looking unto JESUS, THE AUTHOR AND FINISHER OF OUR FAITH; who for the joy that was set before him endured the cross, despising the shame, and is set down at the right hand of the throne of God.*

3. *For consider him that endured such contradiction of sinners against himself, lest ye be wearied and faint in your minds.*

YOUR Bible, is Jesus of Nazareth, in written form," The Author."

Mk. 16:20b
...the Lord working with them, and confirming the word with signs following. Amen.

The "finisher" of our faith. We wouldn't know what to say, if God hadn't given us the promises. We wouldn't know how to speak them into existence if God hadn't taught us how to speak and activate the promise we're standing on and believing for.

Mk. 11:23-24
23. *For verily I say unto you, That whosoever shall say unto this mountain, Be thou removed, and be thou cast into the sea; and shall not doubt in his heart, but shall believe that those things which he saith shall come to pass; he shall have whatsoever he saith.*

24. *THEREFORE I say unto you, What things soever ye desire, when ye pray, BELIEVE THAT YE RECEIVE THEM, AND YE SHALL HAVE THEM.*

Mk. 4:26-29
26. *And he said, So is the kingdom of God, as if a man should cast seed into the ground;*

27. And should sleep, and rise night and day, and the seed should spring and grow up, he knoweth not how.

28. For the earth bringeth forth fruit of herself; first the blade, then the ear, after that the full corn in the ear.

29. But when the fruit is brought forth, immediately he putteth in the sickle, because the harvest is come.

….The seed, is the Word of God or our words based on the Word of God. The soil is the hearts of men. Whether it be the heart of the person you're ministering to, or your own heart,

THE EARTH BRINGETH FORTH FRUIT OF HERSELF!! What you need is not going to come from out there in the world.

The KINGDOM of GOD is inside you. What you want is already inside you. All you need do is Speak it into existence, bringing it into this natural realm.

God can create things out of nothing, and things that already exist.

Like seeds; all the generic information to produce that which does not exist is in the Words themselves. "The substance of things hoped for, the evidence of things not seen."

We, on the other hand, can create things that already exist in the spirit realm and bring them into the natural realm. We are creative beings created in God's image and after His likeness.

Can we, like God create things from nothing? What do you think?

1 Jo. 3:2
Beloved, now are we the sons of God, and it doth not yet appear what we shall be: but we know that, when he shall appear, we shall be like him; for we shall see him as he is.

Put a pair of animals in a valley for 100 years and all you'll end up with is a bunch of animals.

Put a man and woman in the same valley and you'll end up with houses, cars, schools, computers and cell phones. We are creative beings!! Even unbelievers are creative beings, in God's image and after His likeness.

Gen. 22:8
And Abraham said, My son, God will provide himself a lamb for a burnt offering:

….A faith statement? Abraham didn't know anything about the faith doctrine of today.

2 Kgs. 4:26
26. Run now, I pray thee, to meet her, and say unto her, Is it well with thee? is it well with thy husband? is it well with the child? And she answered, IT IS WELL.

Her son was dead. She was hoping that Elisha, could heal her son.

Faith is the substance of things hoped for, the evidence of things not seen,

...but she didn't know the faith message in the Old Testament.

So many people read the Old Testament without the New Testament slant on what they're reading. So many people read the New Testament without The KINGDOM perspective.

Words, are how we live life in The KINGDOM, not money, not silver or gold, or precious stones. It's words only in The KINGDOM of GOD.

How do we buy milk, and bread without money, and without price? In our prayer time with faith filled words accompanied with EXPECTATION, believing what we asked for will happen!!! That's how!!

Why? Because we are His disciples indeed, and we are learning.

●●●●

Day - 4
"Sharper Than Any Two Edged Sword"
(Hebrews 4:12)

Kingdom Seekers
WEEK 2 DAY 4
12-26-2013

We have discussed this before but it is so very important to know and understand that the Word of God now lives inside you.

Gal. 4:6
And because ye are sons, God hath sent forth the Spirit of his Son into your hearts, crying, Abba, Father.

2 Tim. 1:7
For God hath not given us the spirit of fear; but of power, and of love, and of a sound mind.

Yes, the same Word that God released in Genesis, now lives inside you. Jesus is the Word of God personified and He entered into you when you asked Him to save you.

We're not looking at Jesus just now. We're looking at who He was before He was Jesus, He was the Word.

Jo. 1:1-3
1. In the beginning was the Word, and the Word was with God, and the Word was God.
2. The same was in the beginning with God.
3. All things were made by him; and without him was not any thing made that was made.
God framed the creation with the Word…the Word went out and performed the doing of what God said. *(Jo. 1:3 All things were made by him; and without him was not any thing made that was made.)* the carnal minded Christian and the unbeliever are alike in this respect, they build with bricks, mortar, and wood.

The Spirit man which is in right standing with God, builds with words, faith filled words, expecting, until his words come to pass. When the time for the manifestation comes, the bricks, mortar, and wood will be there waiting for him. How exactly does that happen?

Well…Jesus working with us confirming the Word with signs following. *(Mk. 16:20)*

Okay, what makes me think that Jesus would do what I say?

Jo. 14:13-14
13. And whatsoever ye shall ask in my name, that will I do, that the Father may be glorified in the Son.
14. If ye shall ask any thing in my name, I will do it.

When *1 Thes. 5:17* says, Pray without ceasing, the thought is to pray to God in worship, supplication, but also carries the connotation of framing with words…what you would like to have done.

Like praying toward the day your children are ready for college. You just bought your kid's college education without money and without price…at the prayer meeting, with the words of your mouth. IF, your words are accompanied with thought and intent, and you finish your prayer filled with expectation.

(The Word is nigh thee, in thy mouth and in thy heart, that is the Word of faith, which we preach.)

The author and finisher of our faith lives inside you and He said, I WILL DO what you ask in My name!!!

Heb. 4:12
For the word of God is quick, and powerful, and sharper than any twoedged sword, piercing even to the dividing asunder of soul and spirit, and of the joints and marrow, and is a discerner of the thoughts and intents of the heart.

Jesus is in you, He knows what you're thinking, and He knows what you intend to do.

Jam. 4:3
Ye ask, and receive not, because ye ask amiss, that ye may consume it upon your lusts.

Think before you pray. Is it for your carnal lusts, or in line with the Word of God, and righteousness?

When you buy a car, do you pray over it? Do you pray for it's dependability, gas mileage, and traveling mercies? Pray without ceasing toward safety and protection.

Pray for protection when a tornado or ice storm is heading your way.

Pray EXPECTING, that's Faith!!

Jam. 1:17
Every good gift and every perfect gift is from above, and cometh down from the Father of lights, with whom is no variableness, neither shadow of turning.

Do you want your own home? Do you want it to come paid for?

Mk. 4:26-29
26. ...So is the kingdom of God, as if a man should cast seed into the ground;
27. And should sleep, and rise night and day, and the seed should spring and grow up, he knoweth not how.
28. For the earth bringeth forth fruit of herself; first the blade, then the ear, after that the full corn in the ear.
29. But when the fruit is brought forth, immediately he putteth in the sickle, because the harvest is come.

Buy it today without money and without price, then receive it as a done deal!!

You know…I know that sometimes I sound like I'm naïve and gullible but Jesus said, except ye come as little children, ye shall in no wise enter into The KINGDOM of GOD. Little children are teachable and they believe everything they're told.

Of such, is The KINGDOM of GOD. Let's see how the Word works. We'll use "Let there be light," as our example.

Gen. 1:3-4
3. And God said, Let there be light: and there was light.
4. And God saw the light, that it was good:

The Word of God, (which was in God at the time when He spoke those words,) knew what God was thinking and what God intended when God said, "LET THERE BE LIGHT!"

So… the Word, went out into space and created the sun. The Word knew that the sun would not have a solid surface, IT, knew that the sun would give off gamma rays, light rays, ultra violet rays, there would be nuclear fission going on, and solar storms. The Word knew all this and more when God said, "LET THERE BE LIGHT."

Then the Bible says, And God saw the light, that it was good. In other words, it was done right, because the Word knew what God wanted all along.

That same Word is now in you. You have the God given privilege to use His Word, and dictate policy in your own life.

Heb. 10:23
Let us hold fast the profession of our faith without wavering; (for he is faithful that promised;)

Only a King can profess or declare a thing and see it become the law of the land.

Are you one of the Kings that Jesus is King of Kings of? Yes you are! We all are, and we need to learn how to rule in life with Him, by Him, and through Him.

How would you have your life go? Frame it with words, and doubt not in your heart, but believe it will go even as you have said.

Isa. 55:8-11
8. For my thoughts are not your thoughts, neither are your ways my ways, saith the LORD.
9. For as the heavens are higher than the earth, so are my ways higher than your ways, and my thoughts than your thoughts.
10. For as the rain cometh down, and the snow from heaven, and returneth not thither, but watereth the earth, and maketh it bring forth and bud, that it may give seed to the sower, and bread to the eater:
11. So shall my word be that goeth forth out of my mouth: it shall not return unto me void, but it shall accomplish that which I please, and it shall prosper in the thing whereto I sent it.

The Word of God is designed to produce!! What will it, produce? Exactly what it, describes or says.

Then Jesus comes along in John 14, and says, IT, the Word… He, the Word, will do whatsoever we ask in His name, it's His job, it's what He does. He is the Word of God, and He is in you.

He knows if you're believing for what you say or not. He knows, and you can't fool Him.

So go ahead and call those things that be not, as though they were. Bringing into captivity every thought to the obedience of Christ. (The Word) IT, is designed to accomplish. IT, is designed to prosper. Use IT!! He gave IT, to us as a light to our path. Use the promises. Use the Word.

• • • • •

Day - 5
"The Weapons of Our Warfare"
(2 Corinthians 10:4-5)

Kingdom Seekers
WEEK 2 DAY 5
12-27-2013

2 Co. 10:3-5
3. For though we walk in the flesh, we do not war after the flesh:
4. (For the weapons of our warfare are not carnal, but mighty through God to the pulling down of strong holds;)
5. Casting down imaginations, and every high thing that exalteth itself against the knowledge of God, and bringing into captivity every thought to the obedience of Christ;

Eph. 6:12-17
12. For we wrestle not against flesh and blood, but against principalities, against powers, against the rulers of the darkness of this world, against spiritual wickedness in high places.
13. Wherefore take unto you the whole armour of God, that ye may be able to withstand in the evil day, and having done all, to stand.
14. Stand therefore, having your loins girt about with truth, and having on the breastplate of righteousness;
15. And your feet shod with the preparation of the gospel of peace;
16. Above all, taking the shield of faith, wherewith ye shall be able to quench all the fiery darts of the wicked.
17. And take the helmet of salvation, and the sword of the Spirit, which is the word of God:

Okay, that brings us right back to the Word, which is in you. THE DISCERNER, of the thoughts and intents of the heart. Our fight is not with the police department, the school board, the city fathers, or the book return policies at the library. Our fight is with principalities, powers, rulers of darkness of this world, and spiritual wickedness in high places. These are spirits, and spiritual things. Not flesh, and carnal things. You can't go into an elementary school and shoot a spirit, or thwart spiritual wickedness. However, you can speak out against these things with the Sword of the Spirit…words!!

The motivating force of Kingdom Seekers International, is to bring people to the point of "having done all to stand." Then… we can stand, therefore.

I see my job as one who has to change the way you think. If I can change the way you think, YOU will change the way you talk, and words are the only rate of exchange in The KINGDOM of GOD.

What we all need to do; is focus on the real enemy, the devil and his bunch, principalities, powers, rulers of darkness, spiritual wickedness in high places.

Speaking of high things, how about this, the Doctor's report? Your monthly bank statement? These are high things that exault themselves against the knowledge of God. Yoiu should be in need of nothing, no aid, no assistance, no support of any kind, from anyone for anything.

3 Jo. 2
Beloved, I wish above all things that thou mayest prosper and be in health, even as thy soul prospereth.

You know what? I think I have about 5 or 6 people following these teachings so far. Let's say that at the end of the study, there were 200 followers.

Jesus said in
Mk. 4:20
And these are they which are sown on good ground; such as hear the word, and receive it, and bring forth fruit, some thirtyfold, some sixty, and some an hundred.

We are all a product of what we have been taught.

► I see the thirtyfold believer as a person that doesn't know what God's will is for them. They pray, O God, If… it be thy will, do this or that for me. They don't see the promises as the will of God for His people. NO POWER!! The only way to get off the sick list is to die or get over it.

► The sixty-fold believer as a person that believes for the promises, but is walking in limited power, they know it works but they can't explain it, or why it worked for John, but didn't work for Joyce. Again, LIMITED POWER!!

► The hundredfold believer is a person that is learning how to use the power of God, according to the power that worketh in us. They have some successes and experience in the word of truth, and have this confidence,

1 Jo. 5:14-15
14. And this is the confidence that we have in him, that, if we ask any thing according to his will, he heareth us:
15. And if we know that he hear us, whatsoever we ask, we know that we have the petitions that we desired of him.

The hundredfold believer will learn to live out his life according to KINGDOM RULE on the earth. Reigning in life with Christ, by Christ, through Christ, which is The Word of God!!!!

Eph. 4:14-15
14. That we henceforth be no more children, tossed to and fro, and carried about with every wind of doctrine, by the sleight of men, and cunning craftiness, whereby they lie in wait to deceive;
15. But speaking the truth in love, may grow up into him in all things, which is the head, even Christ:

Eph. 4:13
Till we all come in the unity of the faith, and of the knowledge of the Son of God, unto a perfect man, unto the measure of the stature of the fulness of Christ:

We are supposed to grow to the point that we are literally a bunch of little Jesus' walking around on the earth with this attitude, *The Spirit of the Lord is upon me, because he hath anointed me to preach the gospel to the poor; he hath sent me to heal the brokenhearted, to preach deliverance to the captives, and recovering of sight to the blind, to set at liberty them that are bruised, To preach the acceptable year of the Lord.*

What? HOW DARE YOU!!! Well, HOW DARE YOU, resist your calling of the Lord?

Only the hundredfold believer will walk successfully in this calling. As they grow in knowledge, after the image of Him that created him, they will walk in UNLIMITED POWER!!

Of the imaginary 200 followers of this Bible study, many will grow to the sixtyfold position in The KINGDOM. A few, maybe 8 or 10 might grow to the hundredfold position AND become teachers.

I like something I heard a minister say one day, I wish I could grab the top of your head and open it up and pour this into you, but I can't.

Isa. 28:9-11
9. Whom shall he teach knowledge? and whom shall he make to understand doctrine? them that are weaned from the milk, and drawn from the breasts.
10. For precept must be upon precept, precept upon precept; line upon line, line upon line; here a little, and there a little:
11. For with stammering lips and another tongue will he speak to this people.

Why do you think I keep harping on Words, Words, Words? We will be hearing about words throughout the entire course, line upon line, line upon line. Here a little, there a little, here a little, there a little until we drive it down into our spirits, THIS, is how we conduct the business of life in The KINGDOM of GOD.

Okay now, let's start out small. Believe for something that you could easily get for yourself. How about a yellow pencil? Those of you that can believe for a yellow pencil, ask God for one. Okay, let's step it up a little. For those of you that think you have the Faith message under your belt, ask for a pair of socks.

Now…as we say in Oklahoma, you just hide and watch and see if someone or somehow over the next few days, someone brings you, or you find… a yellow pencil. The same with you others, just see over the next few days if someone gives you a pair of socks.

Check it out Bubba, just see if they are the right color you were thinking of.

The Word works!! It'll work every time you put IT to work, IF, you mean what you say!!

He is in you. He knows!

Lock yourself in so tight with your words that you can't wiggle yourself out of this exercise in Faith. This is the victory, even our Faith.

■ ◻ ■

Week-3
Renewing the Mind

Week-3-Days-1-5
Renewing the Mind:
Day-1. Leaving The Principles & Doctrine of Christ. Heb. 6:1-3
Day-2. Renewed in Knowledge. Col. 3:10
Day-3. Be Not Conformed, but Transformed. Ro. 12:2
Day-4. Joint Heirs. Ro. 8:16-17
Day-5. The Heir as Long as He is a Child. Gal. 4:1-3

●

Day - 1
"Leaving The Principles & Doctrine of Christ"
(Hebrews 6:1-3)

Kingdom Seekers
WEEK 3 DAY 1
12-30-2013

Heb. 6:1a
Therefore leaving the principles of the doctrine of Christ, let us go on unto perfection...

As the Lord was giving me this Bible study course, He pointed out that I would have to separate Jesus from the Word. I had a hard time with that because Jesus, IS the Word… personified.

Seeing that I was having trouble with the thought, God took me back to Genesis 1. And showed me how the Word works. Back when the Word was called IT, not Jesus. Yes, when the Word didn't have a name or gender. If the trinity was mentioned in the Old Testament, it would read, The Father, "The Word," and The Holy Spirit. We see the trinity today as The Father, "The Son, and The Holy Spirit. In Genesis "The Word" is not mentioned in that manner.

Isa. 55:10-11
10. For as the rain cometh down, and the snow from heaven, and returneth not thither, but watereth the earth, and maketh it bring forth and bud, that it may give seed to the sower, and bread

to the eater:

11. So shall my word be that goeth forth out of my mouth: it shall not return unto me void, but it shall accomplish that which I please, and it shall prosper in the thing whereto I sent it.

We see two things here.
- 1. The Word is designed to produce or manifest something.
- 2. The Word is called IT. IT, shall accomplish, IT, shall prosper.

We're not talking about Jesus the man right now, we're talking about the "Word." In Proverbs IT, calls Itself Wisdom and understanding. Prv. 7:4. Say unto wisdom, Thou art my sister; and call understanding thy kinswoman: In Genesis, IT had no gender. In Proverbs IT, likened IT'S self to the female gender.

In the beginning was the Word, and the Word was with God, and the Word was God. The same was in the beginning with God. All things were made by him; and without him was not any thing made that was made. And the Word was made flesh, and dwelt among us, …And she shall bring forth a son, and thou shalt call his name JESUS: for he shall save his people from their sins.

Now, the Word, has a name and a gender. We call Him Jesus.

Heb. 6:1a
Therefore leaving the principles of the doctrine of Christ, let us go on unto perfection...

Okay now, we have received Jesus as saviour. Christ, was preached. Now, we need to move on to where the Word is taught. The Word, is who Jesus was before He was Jesus. *(Read Heb. 6:1-20)*

Let's take another look at
Isa. 55:10-11
10. For as the rain cometh down, and the snow from heaven, and returneth not thither, but watereth the earth, and maketh it bring forth and bud, that it may give seed to the sower, and bread to the eater:
11. So shall my word be that goeth forth out of my mouth: it shall not return unto me void, but it shall accomplish that which I please, and it shall prosper in the thing whereto I sent it.

Rain is not designed just to fall, evaporate and then go back up into the atmosphere. It's designed to water the earth so that things can grow. It is designed to produce fruit or a harvest of some kind.

God's Word is designed to do that too. It will not return to Him void, or non-productive. Consider the promises. They are the answers to our needs. When we speak them, believing what we say shall come to pass, they will produce whatsoever we said or described.

Why did I use the word "described"?

Because Jesus said in
Jo. 14:13-14
13. And whatsoever ye shall ask in my name, that will I do, that the Father may be glorified in the Son.
14. If ye shall ask any thing in my name, I will do it.

It's in His job description. It's what He does. He confirms the Word, with signs following. He does everything that God says, and here, He's saying that He will do anything WE say, in His name. What a promise!!

Seeing Jesus as the Word, instead of as the man, opens up a whole new vista of possibility for life in The KINGDOM of GOD.

Lk. 11:9-10
9. And I say unto you, Ask, and it shall be given you; seek, and ye shall find; knock, and it shall be opened unto you.
10. For every one that asketh receiveth; and he that seeketh findeth; and to him that knocketh it shall be opened.

Materialism is quite an issue in the church today. It's root or focus is money. The root of all evil. No wait, the "love" of money, is the root of all evil.

God doesn't mind if you have things. As a mater of fact, He takes great pleasure in the prosperity of His people. When you consider that in The KINGDOM of GOD, we buy without money and without price, the love of money doesn't even enter in to the equation. We use words, accompanied with forethought and intent, to get the things that we want or would like to see happen.

Mt. 10:8
Heal the sick, cleanse the lepers, raise the dead, cast out devils: freely ye have received, freely give.

Jesus was talking about ministry gifts when He said that, but consider this, you asked for that mini van to haul your family around last year. Your kids are in college now. You don't need the van today. Freely ye have received, freely give. Why don't you give the van to that young family in the church that needs it? It didn't cost you a dime when God gave it to you, why not give it to them?

I don't like carnal sayings that the natural mind can understand, but this is an exception.

"If God, can get it through you, He will get it to you."

Can you imagine how it would feel if you were to give a car, a truck or even a home to someone who needs it? Without money and without price?

I know that this sounds too good to be true, but in the Kingdom of God, there are many things that are too good to be true and yet are true!! Set your carnal mind of reason aside for a moment and listen with the mind of your spirit, the mind of Christ. Yes, the mind of Christ!!

Php. 2:3-6
3. Let nothing be done through strife or vainglory; but in lowliness of mind let each esteem other better than themselves.
4. Look not every man on his own things, but every man also on the things of others.
5. Let this mind be in you, which was also in Christ Jesus:
6. Who, being in the form of God, thought it not robbery to be equal with God:

Mt. 17:20
If ye have faith as a grain of mustard seed, ye shall say unto this mountain, Remove hence to yonder place; and it shall remove; and nothing shall be impossible unto you.

Mt. 18:19-20
19. Again I say unto you, That if two of you shall agree on earth as touching any thing that they shall ask, it shall be done for them of my Father which is in heaven.
20. For where two or three are gathered together in my name, there am I in the midst of them.

Mt. 21:21-22
21. Jesus answered and said unto them, Verily I say unto you, If ye have faith, and doubt not, ye shall not only do this which is done to the fig tree, but also if ye shall say unto this mountain, Be thou removed, and be thou cast into the sea; it shall be done.
22. And all things, whatsoever ye shall ask in prayer, believing, ye shall receive.

Mk. 11:24
Therefore I say unto you, What things soever ye desire, when ye pray, believe that ye receive them, and ye shall have them.

Mk. 9:23
Jesus said unto him, If thou canst believe, all things are possible to him that believeth.

••

Day - 2
"Renewed in Knowledge"
(Colossians 3:10)

Kingdom Seekers
WEEK 3 DAY 2
12-31-2013

Col. 3:10
And have put on the new man, which is renewed in knowledge after the image of him that created him:

Eph. 4:21-24
21. If so be that ye have heard him, and have been taught by him, as the truth is in Jesus:
22. That ye put off concerning the former conversation the old man, which is corrupt according to the deceitful lusts;
23. And be renewed in the spirit of your mind;
24. And that ye put on the new man, which after God is created in righteousness and true holiness.

Are you catching the inference here? *(Read: Psa. 139)*

We're not just fearfully and wonderfully made. We're exceedingly, wonderfully made!! With full rights and privileges in the here and now. We don't have to wait for the great by-n-by. We can learn to walk in the power of The KINGDOM today, THIS DAY!!

We saw yesterday,
Php. 2:5-6
5. Let this mind be in you, which was also in Christ Jesus:
6. Who, being in the form of God, thought it not robbery to be equal with God:

No, I don't have the power to heal you. The significance of all this is WE ALL HAVE ACCESS TO THE POWER!! IT'S ACCORDING TO THE POWER THAT WORKETH IN US.

Eph. 3:20
Now unto him that is able to do exceeding abundantly above all that we ask or think, according to the power that worketh in us,

God in Jesus, and Jesus in us, confirming the Word with signs following.

Enough said? No, we need to hear it over and over, line upon line, precept upon precept, here a little, there a little until it gets down into our spirits as a seed.

Only then, will it develop and produce. We don't realize that we are rich beyond measure right now while we're standing in the unemployment line waiting for our weekly check. We do not recognize the true riches because the gospel of The KINGDOM is not being taught in our churches.

Jesus didn't like money!! He called it filthy lucre, and unrighteousness mammon. So He gave us something we could not covet, WORDS!! A never ending inexhaustible supply. We'll never run out of words, no mater what happens, we'll always have something to say about it. The thing is, will we say what the world has taught us to say, or will we say what God has taught us to say?

The world has taught us to say, we're sick and broke and we just can't make it. Nothing ever works out for me, I was born a loser, and I'll die a loser. What's the use? I don't have a chance!!

Father God is teaching us to say other things like, all things are possible to him that believeth and nothing by any means shall hurt us. We can do all things by Christ, who strengthens us. When we are weak, we are strong In His might!!

Hos. 4:6
My people are destroyed for lack of knowledge: because thou hast rejected knowledge, I will also reject thee, that thou shalt be no priest to me: seeing thou hast forgotten the law of thy God, I will also forget thy children.

Mt. 7:7-11
7. Ask, and it shall be given you; seek, and ye shall find; knock, and it shall be opened unto you:
8. For every one that asketh receiveth; and he that seeketh findeth; and to him that knocketh it shall be opened.
9. Or what man is there of you, whom if his son ask bread, will he give him a stone?
10. Or if he ask a fish, will he give him a serpent?
11. If ye then, being evil, know how to give good gifts unto your children, how much more shall your Father which is in heaven give good things to them that ask him?

1 Tim. 4:14-16
14. Neglect not the gift that is in thee, which was given thee by prophecy, with the laying on of the hands of the presbytery.
15. Meditate upon these things; give thyself wholly to them; that thy profiting may appear to all.
16. Take heed unto thyself, and unto the doctrine; continue in them: for in doing this thou shalt both save thyself, and them that hear thee.

Eph. 4:13-15
13. Till we all come in the unity of the faith, and of the knowledge of the Son of God, unto a perfect man, unto the measure of the stature of the fulness of Christ:
14. That we henceforth be no more children, tossed to and fro, and carried about with every

wind of doctrine, by the sleight of men, and cunning craftiness, whereby they lie in wait to deceive;
   15. But speaking the truth in love, may grow up into him in all things, which is the head, even Christ:

No one can renew your mind for you. If you don't do it, it won't get done. You can walk in victory, according to KINGDOM RULE on the earth, or you can just get along and fly by the seat of your pants like the world, who is without God and without hope in the world.

Are you saved? Yes, but listen to this,
Ro. 8:6
For to be carnally minded is death; but to be spiritually minded is life and peace.

This verse is showing us that if you're a believer, but carnally minded, you are symbolically spiritually dead because you won't let God's leading or influence in your life.

Another way of saying it is this, Okay son, if you want to do it your way, you're on your own. He'll work with you as best He can, but life is hard out there in the world. Every time sickness comes, you're going to fall, every time a financial crisis comes, you're going to fall. you're trying to do it the world's way and not God's way.

LIFE IS HARD WITHOUT THE HOLY SPIRIT HELPING US.

God will not over-ride your will. If you insist on doing it your way, OK.

Hey Bud, good luck with that!!

Prv. 1:20-33
20. Wisdom crieth without; she uttereth her voice in the streets:
   21. She crieth in the chief place of concourse, in the openings of the gates: in the city she uttereth her words, saying,
   22. How long, ye simple ones, will ye love simplicity? and the scorners delight in their scorning, and fools hate knowledge?
   23. Turn you at my reproof: behold, I will pour out my spirit unto you, I will make known my words unto you.
   24. Because I have called, and ye refused; I have stretched out my hand, and no man regarded;
   25. But ye have set at nought all my counsel, and would none of my reproof:
   26. I also will laugh at your calamity; I will mock when your fear cometh;
   27. When your fear cometh as desolation, and your destruction cometh as a whirlwind; when distress and anguish cometh upon you.
   28. Then shall they call upon me, but I will not answer; they shall seek me early, but they shall not find me:
   29. For that they hated knowledge, and did not choose the fear of the LORD:
   30. They would none of my counsel: they despised all my reproof.
   31. Therefore shall they eat of the fruit of their own way, and be filled with their own devices.

32. For the turning away of the simple shall slay them, and the prosperity of fools shall destroy them.
33. But whoso hearkeneth unto me shall dwell safely, and shall be quiet from fear of evil.

You have a choice today. Are you going to continue to resist God's influence in your life? Or are you going to submit to His direction in your life?

He wants to help. He's standing at the ready to abound toward you with immeasurable blessings. The promises were given, the works were finished from thr foundation of the world for us to walk in.

Deut. 30:19
I call heaven and earth to record this day against you, that I have set before you life and death, blessing and cursing: therefore choose life, that both thou and thy seed may live:

● ● ●

Day - 3
"Be Not Conformed, but Transformed"
(Romans 12:2)

Kingdom Seekers
WEEK 3 DAY 3
01-01-2014

Romans 12:2
And be not conformed to this world: but be ye transformed by the renewing of your mind, that ye may prove what is that good, and acceptable, and perfect, will of God.

...as I mentioned before, if I don't renew my mind from the worlds ways to God's ways, my mind will not be renewed. God is a gentleman, He will not over-ride my will and force me to get in line with His instructions. This is a job or process that we must do ourselves. Once we set our hearts and minds to it, He will help. Until then, we are on our own!

Being a child when we receive Jesus as saviour is far better than a person of say 50 years old. A child hasn't yet learned the ways of the world. An adult has to ignore his past experiences in the world and learn the ways of God. That's a much harder process. Even if a child receives Jesus at a young age, if he or she is not trained in the ways of the Kingdom, they will probably learn the ways of the world before he learns the ways of God.

Therefore, we have the battle of the minds. The mind of reason against the mind of the Spirit.

We see in Ro. 12:2, That we are to prove what is that good, acceptable, and perfect will of God.

How do we find out what God's will is? THE PROMISES!! The promises are the answers to all our needs.

Eph. 3:9
And to make all men see what is the fellowship of the mystery, which from the beginning of the world hath been hid in God, who created all things by Jesus Christ:

1 Jo. 6:14-15
14. And this is the confidence that we have in him, that, if we ask any thing according to his will, he heareth us:
15. And if we know that he hear us, whatsoever we ask, we know that we have the petitions that we desired of him.

Look at
1 Jo. 5:13
These things have I written unto you that believe on the name of the Son of God; that ye may know that ye have eternal life, and that ye may believe on the name of the Son of God.

Sounds a little redundant doesn't it? Now that you have believed on the name of the Son of God, you may now, believe on the name of the Son of God!!

What's he saying here? Now that you have believed on the name for salvation, you may now believe on that name as a way of life, from faith to faith, for the just shall live by Faith.

When you have a need, find a promise that covers that need, speak it, doubt not in your heart, but believe what you said shall come to pass. Isn't that what Jesus said?

Yeah but, what if you can't find a promise to cover your need? Okay, no problem, we have some exceeding great and precious promises available to us.

Mt. 21:21-22
21. Jesus answered and said unto them, Verily I say unto you, If ye have faith, and doubt not, ye shall not only do this which is done to the fig tree, but also if ye shall say unto this mountain, Be thou removed, and be thou cast into the sea; it shall be done.
22. And all things, whatsoever ye shall ask in prayer, believing, ye shall receive.

Mk. 11:23-24
23. For verily I say unto you, That whosoever shall say unto this mountain, Be thou removed, and be thou cast into the sea; and shall not doubt in his heart, but shall believe that those things which he saith shall come to pass; he shall have whatsoever he saith.
24. Therefore I say unto you, What things soever ye desire, when ye pray, believe that ye receive them, and ye shall have them.

Lk. 17:6
And the Lord said, If ye had faith as a grain of mustard seed, ye might say unto this sycamine tree, Be thou plucked up by the root, and be thou planted in the sea; and it should obey you.

Jo. 14:13-14
13. And whatsoever ye shall ask in my name, that will I do, that the Father may be glorified in the Son.
14. If ye shall ask any thing in my name, I will do it.

Jo. 15:7
If ye abide in me, and my words abide in you, ye shall ask what ye will, and it shall be done unto you.

Jo. 16:23-24
23. And in that day ye shall ask me nothing. Verily, verily, I say unto you, Whatsoever ye shall ask the Father in my name, he will give it you.
24. Hitherto have ye asked nothing in my name: ask, and ye shall receive, that your joy may be full.

2 Pet. 1:11
For so an entrance shall be ministered unto you abundantly into the everlasting kingdom of our Lord and Saviour Jesus Christ.

Col. 1:13
Who hath delivered us from the power of darkness, and hath translated us into the kingdom of his dear Son:

Every thing you have learned in the world will serve you no purpose in The KINGDOM of GOD. In The KINGDOM of GOD, we don't need tools and equipment, money or supplies like lumber, concrete, or nails.

All we need are Words. Our Words will do our bidding for us in all things.

Again...
Jo. 14:13-14
13. And whatsoever ye shall ask in my name, that will I do, that the Father may be glorified in the Son.
14. If ye shall ask any thing in my name, I will do it.

Jesus is the Word. It's in His job description to perform the doing of what God says...

And now...what We say, believing we receive as we pray.

Jo. 16:24
Hitherto have ye asked nothing in my name: ask, and ye shall receive, that your joy may be full.

God has done a multitude of things for us, but there are several things that God has told us to do. Be not conformed to this world is one, and to renew our minds is another. If we don't do it, it won't get done.

Why?

Because it's our responsibility.

Obviously, these are things that the devil doesn't want us to know.

2 Pet. 1:11
For so an entrance shall be ministered unto you abundantly into the everlasting kingdom of our Lord and Saviour Jesus Christ.

Lk. 12:32.
Fear not, little flock; for it is your Father's good pleasure to give you the kingdom.

●●●●

Day - 4
"Joint Heirs"
(Romans 8:16-17)

Kingdom Seekers
WEEK 3 DAY 4
01-02-2014

Ro. 8:16-17
16. The Spirit itself beareth witness with our spirit, that we are the children of God:
17. And if children, then heirs; heirs of God, and joint-heirs with Christ; if so be that we suffer with him, that we may be also glorified together.

The Spirit itself...
Gal. 4:6
And because ye are sons, God hath sent forth the Spirit of his Son into your hearts, crying, Abba, Father.

Joint heirs with Christ….this is not a separation of estate. Jesus gets this part, Peter gets that part, Paul gets the other part.

No, we all share the whole of the inheritance.

Heb. 1:1-2
1. God, who at sundry times and in divers manners spake in time past unto the fathers by the prophets,
2. Hath in these last days spoken unto us by his Son, [whom he hath appointed heir of all things,] by whom also he made the worlds;

Jesus is the appointed heir of all things and we are joint heirs with Him… of all things!!

Well…you say, that is speaking of Spiritual things, not material things. Oh?

The Bible says that Abraham was very rich in cattle, silver, and gold. Don't cut yourself short.

Jesus said in
Mk. 4:23-24
23. If any man have ears to hear, let him hear.
24. And he said unto them, Take heed what ye hear: with what measure ye mete, it shall be measured to you: and unto you that hear shall more be given.

If you measure all things to be Spiritual, then Spiritual… is all you're going to get.

1 Tim. 6:17-18
17. Charge them that are rich in this world, that they be not highminded, nor trust in uncertain riches, but in the living God, who giveth us richly all things to enjoy;
18. That they do good, that they be rich in good works, ready to distribute, willing to communicate;

Come on now, do you honestly think that rich people can buy Spiritual things?

I don't think so!! One fella named Simon, found that out in Acts 8:20.

Since money is not going to be involved, ask what you will, and it shall be done unto you. Isn't that what Jesus said, in Jo. 15:7?

Don't try it…DO IT!!

Do you want a hang-glider? Ask for one, believe you receive it as you ask, doubt not in your heart, and you shall have one. Not only have one, but also He will give you the grace to handle it without scratches, bruises, or broken bones. All things to enjoy!! When you're through with it, give it to someone who wants one. Pray and agree that they too, won't end up with scratches, bruises, or broken bones.

All things to enjoy!!

Jas. 2:5
Hearken, my beloved brethren, Hath not God chosen the poor of this world rich in faith, and heirs of the kingdom which he hath promised to them that love him?

Mk. 10:23-25
23. And Jesus looked round about, and saith unto his disciples, How hardly shall they that have riches enter into the kingdom of God!
24. And the disciples were astonished at his words. But Jesus answereth again, and saith unto them, Children, how hard is it for them that trust in riches to enter into the kingdom of God!
25. It is easier for a camel to go through the eye of a needle, than for a rich man to enter into the kingdom of God.

The love of money is the root of all evil. In The Kingdom of GOD, we do not deal with money, we live... by our words, we receive... by our words, we acquire... by our words!! The true riches are WORDS!!

We are joint heirs of all things. Things Spiritual, things material, things pertaining to life and Godliness, things emotional. All things to enjoy!!

Jo. 10:10
The thief cometh not, but for to steal, and to kill, and to destroy: I am come that they might have life, and that they might have it more abundantly.

Jo. 14:6
Jesus saith unto him, I am the way, the truth, and the life: no man cometh unto the Father, but by me.

Gal. 4:1-7
1. Now I say, That the heir, as long as he is a child, differeth nothing from a servant, though he be lord of all;
2. But is under tutors and governors until the time appointed of the father.
3. Even so we, when we were children, were in bondage under the elements of the world:
4. But when the fulness of the time was come, God sent forth his Son, made of a woman, made under the law,
5. To redeem them that were under the law, that we might receive the adoption of sons.
6. And because ye are sons, God hath sent forth the Spirit of his Son into your hearts, crying, Abba, Father.
7. Wherefore thou art no more a servant, but a son; and if a son, then an heir of God through Christ.

As long as we are children, we are subject to tutors and governors "teachers," and are in bondage of the elements of the world, until the time appointed of the Father. In other words, until we grow up in the knowledge of Him that created us.

Through this simple Bible study we are being taught "having done all to stand"!!

Remember...

Eph. 6:13-14

13. Wherefore take unto you the whole armour of God, that ye may be able to withstand in the evil day, "and having done all, to stand."

14. "Stand therefore," having your loins girt about with truth, and having on the breastplate of righteousness;

(v. 12) For we wrestle not against flesh and blood, but against principalities, against powers, against the rulers of the darkness of this world, against spiritual wickedness in high places.

How do we do this?

2 Co. 10:3-5

3. For though we walk in the flesh, we do not war after the flesh:

4. (For the weapons of our warfare are not carnal, but mighty through God to the pulling down of strong holds;)

5. Casting down imaginations, and every high thing that exalteth itself against the knowledge of God, and bringing into captivity every thought to the obedience of Christ;

How do we know this will work?

Mk. 16:20

And they went forth, and preached every where, "the Lord working with them, and confirming the word with signs following. Amen."

1 Jo. 3:2-9

2. Beloved, now are we the sons of God, and it doth not yet appear what we shall be: but we know that, when he shall appear, we shall be like him; for we shall see him as he is.

3. And every man that hath this hope in him purifieth himself, even as he is pure.

4. Whosoever committeth sin transgresseth also the law: for sin is the transgression of the law.

5. And ye know that he was manifested to take away our sins; and in him is no sin.

6. Whosoever abideth in him sinneth not: whosoever sinneth hath not seen him, neither known him.

7. Little children, let no man deceive you: he that doeth righteousness is righteous, even as he is righteous.

8. He that committeth sin is of the devil; for the devil sinneth from the beginning. For this purpose the Son of God was manifested, that he might destroy the works of the devil.

9. Whosoever is born of God doth not commit sin; for his seed remaineth in him: and he cannot sin, because he is born of God.

We are fearfully and wonderfully made in Christ. Not apart from Him, but in Him. We will be given glorified bodies just like His. We will reign in life with Him just as soon,… as we learn how.

That's what Kingdom Seekers is all about, learning how to live life on the earth according to

KINGDOM RULE, not like the rest of mankind, just trying to make the best of a bad situation. Life is hard outside The KINGDOM of GOD.

Mt. 11:28-30
28. Come unto me, all ye that labour and are heavy laden, and I will give you rest.
29. Take my yoke upon you, and learn of me; for I am meek and lowly in heart: and ye shall find rest unto your souls.
30. For my yoke is easy, and my burden is light.

● ● ● ● ●

Day - 5
"The Heir as Long as He is a Child"
(Galatians 4:1-3)

Kingdom Seekers
WEEK 3 DAY 5
01-03-2014

Gal. 4:1-7
1. Now I say, That the heir, as long as he is a child, differeth nothing from a servant, though he be lord of all;
2. But is under tutors and governors until the time appointed of the father.
3. Even so we, when we were children, were in bondage under the elements of the world:
4. But when the fulness of the time was come, God sent forth his Son, made of a woman, made under the law,
5. To redeem them that were under the law, that we might receive the adoption of sons.
6. And because ye are sons, God hath sent forth the Spirit of his Son into your hearts, crying, Abba, Father.
7. Wherefore thou art no more a servant, but a son; and if a son, then an heir of God through Christ.

We touched on this yesterday but we need to take a closer look at these scriptures because they give us a lot of information. We need to know why sickness, disease and financial ruin are rampant in the church right now, and we need to know how to overcome it.

● (v.1) *Now I say, That the heir, as long as he is a child, differeth nothing from a servant, though he be lord of all;*

Let's use a business as an example. A business owner had a child a few years ago. The child Johnny, is now nine years old. Dad brought Johnny to work one day and Johnny was fascinated with the production line.

Johnny said, "It would be neat if that piece of equipment were over in the corner beside that other one, the production line would work smoother that way."

The foreman of course listened to him and said, "I'll tell that to my supervisor and sent Johnny on his way."

The foreman didn't mention the idea to anyone.

Why?

Because this was just a little child. He doesn't know anything about the business or how to run it. So, his suggestion goes unheeded.

Now when Johnny is 15, and makes a suggestion like that, the foreman listens a little closer but still doesn't do anything because Johnny has no authority, but he may pass the suggestion on to the business owner.

Now Johnny is 21. The foreman knows that it won't be long till Johnny takes over the business. Every suggestion is considered.

Why?

Because Johnny knows the business process and wants to improve production.

Okay, for the sake of argument, let's say the foreman is the god of this world, satan, and the workers are the demons under his control. As long as Johnny was a child, the workers didn't listen to him, even laughed at him whether his suggestions were good or not.

As an adolescent, they were suspicious and wary of him, wondering what he knew. They would attack him emotionally, and rebuke him at every opportunity, even cause him illness and pain, and keep him financially strapped to the point that he couldn't do anything.

Now… he is a man. He's taking over the Father's business. The workers now know that he knows who he is and what his job is.

My point is this…once the devil knows that YOU know who you are in Christ, he will back off for a season like he did with Jesus. Like a snake, he will try to attack you from time to time.

As a mature Christian, we will be able to thwart all attempts to blindside us and demoralize us and defeat us in any way.

Eph. 6:10-17
10. Finally, my brethren, be strong in the Lord, and in the power of his might.

11. Put on the whole armour of God, that ye may be able to stand against the wiles of the devil.

12. For we wrestle not against flesh and blood, but against principalities, against powers, against the rulers of the darkness of this world, against spiritual wickedness in high places.

13. Wherefore take unto you the whole armour of God, that ye may be able to withstand in the evil day, and having done all, to stand.

14. Stand therefore, having your loins girt about with truth, and having on the breastplate of righteousness;

15. And your feet shod with the preparation of the gospel of peace;

16. Above all, taking the shield of faith, wherewith ye shall be able to quench all the fiery darts of the wicked.

17. And take the helmet of salvation, and the sword of the Spirit, which is the word of God:

• (v.2) *But is under tutors and governors until the time appointed of the father.*

…this doesn't mean July 10th. It means when an individual reaches spiritual awareness, and maturity. Then…we will walk in the power of The KINGDOM, ruling and reigning in life with Christ.

• (v.3) *Even so we, when we were children, were in bondage under the elements of the world:*

1 Co. 13:11-12

11. When I was a child, I spake as a child, I understood as a child, I thought as a child: but when I became a man, I put away childish things.

12. For now we see through a glass, darkly; but then face to face: now I know in part; but then shall I know even as also I am known.

The elements of the world…. The curse of the law is still out there. As we saw earlier, we started in the Spirit, but when we tried to go back and do the "works of the law" we put ourselves back under the curse, even though we are redeemed from the curse, we put ourselves back subject to the curse.

As long as we don't know who we are in Christ, the devil as a roaring lion seeks those that he can overcome and devour them. Or as Jesus said it to Peter…sift them as wheat.

Gal. 4:4-5

4. But when the fulness of the time was come, God sent forth his Son, made of a woman, made under the law,

5. To redeem them that were under the law, that we might receive the adoption of sons.

Jesus came and died for our sins, was buried, and resurrected again. We are all born-again "IN HIM." Joint heirs with Him. Not co-heirs, as in we all get a portion, but joint heirs. With Jesus, we get it all!!

● (v.6) *And because ye are sons, God hath sent forth the Spirit of his Son into your hearts, crying, Abba, Father.*

We have His Word, His Name, and His Spirit. If God be for us, who can be against us?

———————

Next week could be a most exciting week for the Kingdom Realities Bible Study Course. We're going to learn how to talk!!

Weeks 4 and 5 are going to be most enlightening.

When we were born of Mom and Dad, we were born with a mind. It was empty, but we had one. It took awhile but we did learn how to walk and talk.

Jesus said, "My words, they are Spirit and they are life."

When we were born again of God, we were born with a mind. It was empty, but we had one. Let's learn how to talk so that our words, they are Spirit and they are life!!

▶ **Week-4. Exact Knowledge.**
▶ **Week-5. God's thoughts and Ways.**
▶ **Week-6. Walk as Children of Light.**

Jesus said it repeatedly, If any man have ears to hear, let him hear!!

Do you remember what He said about the eunuch?

Mt. 19:11-12
11. But he said unto them, All men cannot receive this saying, save they to whom it is given.
12. For there are some eunuchs, which were so born from their mother's womb: and there are some eunuchs, which were made eunuchs of men: and there be eunuchs, which have made themselves eunuchs for the kingdom of heaven's sake. He that is able to receive it, let him receive it.

I may lose some of you over the next few weeks.

■ ◻ ■ ◻

Week-4
Exact Knowledge

Week-4-Days-1-5
Exact Knowledge:

●

Day - 1
"Man's Wisdom / God's Knowledge"
(James 3:15-17)

Kingdom Seekers
WEEK 4 DAY 1
01-06-2014

Jas. 3:13-18
13. Who is a wise man and endued with knowledge among you? let him show out of a good conversation his works with meekness of wisdom.
14. But if ye have bitter envying and strife in your hearts, glory not, and lie not against the truth.
15. This wisdom descendeth not from above, but is earthly, sensual, devilish.
16. For where envying and strife is, there is confusion and every evil work.
17. But the wisdom that is from above is first pure, then peaceable, gentle, and easy to be entreated, full of mercy and good fruits, without partiality, and without hypocrisy.
18. And the fruit of righteousness is sown in peace of them that make peace.

Earthly, sensual, devilish!!

▶EARTHLY: Man's knowledge changes every time a university does a new study. Knowledge is updated and old knowledge passes away. No longer valid, no longer true, no longer "the way it is today." Because we have learned more about it. Man's knowledge is iffy at best!!

► SENSUAL: Man's knowledge is centered toward the five physical senses. It could be categorized as, "The Lust of," the Flesh, the Mind, the Touch, the Taste, the Smell, the Sound, and the Eye.

► DEVILISH: The devil cannot create. However, he can distort, and pervert what God has created. His favorite game is, "YEA, HATH GOD NOT SAID?" He used it with Eve, in the garden, and he used it with Jesus. "IF…thou be the Son of God".….

Don't be stupid.

God has made a way for us. Jesus said, I am the Way, the Truth, and the Life!! But wait, who was Jesus before He was Jesus?

Let's state that verse this way. The Word, is the Way, the Truth, and the Life!! Jesus is the Word of God, personified.

When we agree in prayer with someone and quote scripture, He is there in the midst. If we are believing for what we agreed on, He will perform the doing of the agreement. If we aren't believing for what we agreed on, Jesus is not obligated to confirm our words…with signs following.

That's why I say, if you're hoping and EXPECTING, after you pray, that's FAITH, And you're going to get whatever you're believing for.

Heb. 11:1
Now faith is the substance of things hoped for, the evidence of things not seen.

1 Co. 1:24-31
24. But unto them which are called, both Jews and Greeks, Christ the power of God, and the wisdom of God.
25. Because the foolishness of God is wiser than men; and the weakness of God is stronger than men.
26. For ye see your calling, brethren, how that not many wise men after the flesh, not many mighty, not many noble, are called:
27. But God hath chosen the foolish things of the world to confound the wise; and God hath chosen the weak things of the world to confound the things which are mighty;
28. And base things of the world, and things which are despised, hath God chosen, yea, and things which are not, to bring to nought things that are:
29. That no flesh should glory in his presence.
30. But of him are ye in Christ Jesus, who of God is made unto us wisdom, and righteousness, and sanctification, and redemption:
31. That, according as it is written, He that glorieth, let him glory in the Lord.

[Christ the power of God, and the wisdom of God.] God has placed His power in words themselves. Like seeds, they are able to produce what they say, or describe.

Isa. 55:10-11

10. For as the rain cometh down, and the snow from heaven, and returneth not thither, but watereth the earth, and maketh it bring forth and bud, that it may give seed to the sower, and bread to the eater:

11. So shall my word be that goeth forth out of my mouth: it shall not return unto me void, but it shall accomplish that which I please, and it shall prosper in the thing whereto I sent it.

By whose stripes we were healed, is designed to produce healing for us. Is that too far out to understand?

1 Co. 2:1-7

1. And I, brethren, when I came to you, came not with excellency of speech or of wisdom, declaring unto you the testimony of God.

2. For I determined not to know any thing among you, save Jesus Christ, and him crucified.

3. And I was with you in weakness, and in fear, and in much trembling.

4. And my speech and my preaching was not with enticing words of man's wisdom, but in demonstration of the Spirit and of power:

5. That your faith should not stand in the wisdom of men, but in the power of God.

6. Howbeit we speak wisdom among them that are perfect: yet not the wisdom of this world, nor of the princes of this world, that come to nought:

7. But we speak the wisdom of God in a mystery, even the hidden wisdom, which God ordained before the world unto our glory:

(v.4b) ...demonstration of the Spirit and of power: (v.5) That your faith should not stand in the wisdom of men, but in the power of God.

If you're not getting results, it's because you're not doing it right. There should be demonstration of the Spirit and of power in your words, that your faith should not stand in the wisdom of men, but in the power of God.

Your words need to be accompanied with thought and intent because

Heb. 4:12

For the word of God is quick, and powerful, and sharper than any twoedged sword, piercing even to the dividing asunder of soul and spirit, and of the joints and marrow, and is a discerner of the thoughts and intents of the heart.

The Word is in you, He knows your thoughts and intents. If you're believing for what you prayed for, you're going to get it. If you're not, the Word is not obligated to confirm your words with signs following.

Why did I say...YOUR WORDS?

Jo. 14:13-14

13. And whatsoever ye shall ask in my name, that will I do, that the Father may be glorified in the Son.

14. If ye shall ask any thing in my name, I WILL DO IT.

Ro. 8:5-8

5. For they that are after the flesh do mind the things of the flesh; but they that are after the Spirit the things of the Spirit.

6. For to be carnally minded is death; but to be spiritually minded is life and peace.

7. Because the carnal mind is enmity against God: for it is not subject to the law of God, neither indeed can be.

8. So then they that are in the flesh cannot please God.

1 Co. 2:12-14

12. Now we have received, not the spirit of the world, but the spirit which is of God; that we might know the things that are freely given to us of God.

13. Which things also we speak, not in the words which man's wisdom teacheth, but which the Holy Ghost teacheth; comparing spiritual things with spiritual.

14. But the natural man receiveth not the things of the Spirit of God: for they are foolishness unto him: neither can he know them, because they are spiritually discerned.

———

I have been asked if anyone can get all the Daily messages at one time. Yes, just go to my face book page "Jerry Hollenbeck" where you will find them all. If you can't get to that page, send me a friend request and I will accept your request.

●●

Day - 2
"If You Continue in My Word"
(John 8:32)

Kingdom Seekers
WEEK 4 DAY 2
01-07-2014

Jo. 8:31-32

31. Then said Jesus to those Jews which believed on him, If ye continue in my word, then are ye my disciples indeed;

32. And ye shall know the truth, and the truth shall make you free.

The main purpose of this Bible study is to research the Bible and find out who we are, then develop the truths we find into our spirits so that we can live the overcoming life that God has prepared for us.

I use the example of a horse-colt when he is born, he already has everything he will ever need to be a champion in his field. Whether he be a draft horse, a Tennessee walker, a Quarter horse, or a Thoroughbred race horse, he already has everything he needs. It only needs to be developed. That's why horse owners send their colts to trainers, to be trained, and develop the qualities they already have in them.

Was Jesus talking only to His disciples?

No, He was talking also to those who believed on Him. There could have been 100 people standing there that day.

Now then, here's a perfect example of what I've been saying over and over throughout this study. The Word of God is designed to produce itself, "whatsoever it says or describes" And ye shall know the truth, and the truth shall make you free. Let's look at it in it's best illustration.

Isa. 55:10-11
10. For as the rain cometh down, and the snow from heaven, and returneth not thither, but watereth the earth, and maketh it bring forth and bud, that it may give seed to the sower, and bread to the eater:
11. So shall my word be that goeth forth out of my mouth: it shall not return unto me void, but it shall accomplish that which I please, and it shall prosper in the thing whereto I sent it.

"By whose stripes ye were healed" is designed to effect healing for us if we speak it, doubt not in our hearts, but believe what we said shall come to pass!! And the saying will heal us because God watches over His Word to perform it, Jesus also working with us confirming the Word, with signs following, God also bearing witness with signs and wonders, and divers miracles.

We've all heard it over and over, God doesn't have any problem with us believing Him, what He has a problem with, is us "declaring what we believe" in order to effect a change in our circumstances!! It's not the believing, it's the saying. That's where we miss it!! We need to say what we believe, "expecting," until what we said comes to pass. THAT'S LIVING BY FAITH.

IF YOU'RE NOT EXPECTING, then Jesus, is not obligated to confirm our words with signs following.

Got it? It's as simple as that!! Without Faith, it is impossible to please God.

Okay, let's see it again, what do we say, and how do we say it?

Okay….

Mk. 4:14-15

14. The sower soweth the word.

15. And these are they by the way side, where the word is sown; but when they have heard, Satan cometh immediately, and taketh away the word that was sown in their hearts.

The seed, is the word of God. The soil, is the hearts of men. We are God's husbandry, He sows His Word into us. We are made of the earth. The Word of God entered into us, and quickened us and made our dead spirits alive of His incorruptible seed. The Word entered into us, (our body which is made of the earth) quickened our spirit, (which is made without hands) and we are born in righteousness and true holiness, of incorruptible seed.

Now, being a child of God, we have rights and privileges we didn't have before. We have His word, His Spirit, and His Name, and the right to use them against the tests and trials, circumstances and situations that seem to come in on every wave.

If ye have faith as a grain of mustard seed, ye shall say unto this mountain, Remove hence to yonder place; and it shall remove; and nothing shall be impossible unto you.

Find a promise that covers your need, speak it, doubt not in your heart, but believe what you said shall come to pass. If you'll do that, you shall have exactly what you said!!

But that's not all. We can speak God's promises with full assurance and Jesus said in

Jo. 14:13-14

13. And whatsoever ye shall ask in my name, that will I do, that the Father may be glorified in the Son.

14. If ye shall ask any thing in my name, I will do it.

So…we can say what God has said about us to help us in time of need, and we can speak in our own words, how we would have things be. Yes, we can dictate policy in our own lives, as we will….according to the Word of God.

If you really knew what is available to us as children of The Most High God, why would you ask God to help you with the down payment for that new house, when you could ask Him for a house and to have it come paid for?

Have you ever heard of preventive maintenance? Replace that old tire before you have a blowout on the road at 70 mph, or "pay it forward"?

Ask for your new house NOW, when you can't hardly make ends meet every month. Buy it NOW, in your prayer time "without money and without price."

Jas. 1:17
Every good gift and every perfect gift is from above, and cometh down from the Father of lights, with whom is no variableness, neither shadow of turning.

When the manifestation comes, you will not only have your house, but it will come without a mortgage.

Yes, but how can I guarantee that?

I can't…Jesus is our guarantee!! "Whatsoever ye shall ask in My name, I WILL DO IT!!"

I'm not saying that it won't take money to buy the house when the time comes. I'm just saying that when the time comes, the money will be there waiting for you.

This is impossible in the natural world!! However, this is the way things are done in the Kingdom of God.

We "declare with our words" what we want, and the Word, produces it.

1 Jo. 5:13-15
13. These things have I written unto you that believe on the name of the Son of God; that ye may know that ye have eternal life, and that ye may believe on the name of the Son of God.
14. And this is the confidence that we have in him, that, if we ask any thing according to his will, he heareth us:
15. And if we know that he hear us, whatsoever we ask, we know that we have the petitions that we desired of him.

Where is your confidence level? In what the world has taught you, or in what God is teaching you? Line upon line, line upon line, precept upon precept, precept upon precept, here a little, there a little.

Jesus said, My words, they are spirit and they are life. We need to learn to speak from our spirits and not from the carnal mind of reason.

Jo. 10:10
The thief cometh not, but for to steal, and to kill, and to destroy: I am come that they might have life, and that they might have it more abundantly.

You already have all the wealth you will ever need, speak the Word only, and you shall have what you say.

Greed, doesn't even enter into the equation, there is no money involved in the issues of life, in The KINGDOM of GOD.

Words only, and words are free of cost for us. Jesus paid the cost for our lives on the cross. We are free, joint heirs with Christ, NOW, in this world. Everything He has is our's, right now. We don't have to wait for the great by-n-by. Abundant life, abundant health, abundant wealth, right now!! We need to keep our requests limited to the Word of God, by His Promises, Truths, Spiritual Laws and Righteousness. Other than that, we are only limited to our own imagination.

What do you want? Speak it, doubt not, but believe you will have it.

Of course I couldn't ask for a woman to divorce her husband so that I could have her, That's against Bible teaching.

But literally, what do you want? Ask for it, believe you receive it, and go on about your business as though it's a done deal. Because it is!!

It is said that a man asked a great man of God once, you have been teaching Mk. 11:23 for 60 years now. When are you going to move on to something else?

The man of God answered, when you get it, I'll move on to something else.

We need to get this into our spirits, the monetary value in The KINGDOM of GOD is not money!! It's words only!! Words directed…with forethought and intent!!

● ● ●

Day - 3
"The True Riches"
(Luke 16:10-12)

Kingdom Seekers
WEEK 4 DAY 3
01-08-2014

Lk. 16:10-13
10. He that is faithful in that which is least is faithful also in much: and he that is unjust in the least is unjust also in much.
11. If therefore ye have not been faithful in the unrighteous mammon, who will commit to your trust the true riches?
12. And if ye have not been faithful in that which is another man's, who shall give you that which is your own?
13. No servant can serve two masters: for either he will hate the one, and love the other; or else he will hold to the one, and despise the other. Ye cannot serve God and mammon.

Unrighteous mammon,wow Jesus didn't have much good to say about money.

Ezek. 28:11-19

11. Moreover the word of the LORD came unto me, saying,

12. Son of man, take up a lamentation upon the king of Tyrus, and say unto him, Thus saith the Lord GOD; Thou sealest up the sum, full of wisdom, and perfect in beauty.

13. Thou hast been in Eden the garden of God; every precious stone was thy covering, the sardius, topaz, and the diamond, the beryl, the onyx, and the jasper, the sapphire, the emerald, and the carbuncle, and gold: the workmanship of thy tabrets and of thy pipes was prepared in thee in the day that thou wast created.

14. Thou art the anointed cherub that covereth; and I have set thee so: thou wast upon the holy mountain of God; thou hast walked up and down in the midst of the stones of fire.

15. Thou wast perfect in thy ways from the day that thou wast created, till iniquity was found in thee.

16. By the multitude of thy merchandise they have filled the midst of thee with violence, and thou hast sinned: therefore I will cast thee as profane out of the mountain of God: and I will destroy thee, O covering cherub, from the midst of the stones of fire.

17. Thine heart was lifted up because of thy beauty, thou hast corrupted thy wisdom by reason of thy brightness: I will cast thee to the ground, I will lay thee before kings, that they may behold thee.

18. Thou hast defiled thy sanctuaries by the multitude of thine iniquities, by the iniquity of thy traffic; therefore will I bring forth a fire from the midst of thee, it shall devour thee, and I will bring thee to ashes upon the earth in the sight of all them that behold thee.

19. All they that know thee among the people shall be astonished at thee: thou shalt be a terror, and never shalt thou be any more.

"By the multitude of thy merchandise" …Lucifer, was consumed with his wealth and knowledge. The anointed cherub that covereth. He was self deceived. He tried to move God aside and take His place… Bad idea!!

The love of money. The root of all evil. Ironically, God created an entire race of beings, and gave us what the devil tried to take. Money was the rate of exchange on the earth in those days. However, in The KINGDOM of GOD, on the earth as well as in heaven, money was replaced with God's rate of exchange, Words!! Words, just like a seed, are able to produce what they say or describe. IF…they're said right!! Full of love, faith, forethought, and intent. In other words, we need to mean what we say, and stand ready to back our words up, because Jesus is standing at the ready, prepared to back us up. Jesus is our surety, our guarantee.

Jo. 14:13-14

13. And whatsoever ye shall ask in my name, that will I do, that the Father may be glorified in the Son.

14. If ye shall ask any thing in my name, I will do it.

We see this promise in verse 13, then reiterated in verse 14, and we still don't take Jesus at His Word.

What's the matter with our ability to think?

I'll tell you what the matter is, the carnal mind can't reason it out, it's too good to be true!! Yes, it is too good to be true in the natural, but IT IS TRUE in The KINGDOM of GOD!! Using Words, that's how we get things done in The KINGDOM.

Wouldn't it be great if Jesus would have told us what the true riches are?

But this is hidden information, hidden wisdom, that comes only by revelation from the Spirit of God to our spirits. The thing is, when we receive the revelation, old familiar scripture suddenly takes on a new dynamic to them. *Mt. 17:20; 21:21-22, Mk. 11:23-24, Lk. 17:6, Jo. 14:13-14; 15:7; 16:23-24.* All these verses suddenly make perfect sense when we see that true riches don't come in the form of money, but in the form of words.

Primarily God's word, in the form of the promises given to us.

Then, the Word Himself, came along in
Jo. 14:13-14
13. And whatsoever ye shall ask in my name, that will I do, that the Father may be glorified in the Son.
14. If ye shall ask any thing in my name, I will do it.

So we have God's words and our own words. We have been taught how to speak...... Believing we receive.....as we are speaking!!

Are you getting a feeling in your spirit that you have heard this before? We've all heard it before. Watch your words, they have the ability to bring themselves to pass. Guard the words of your mouth. Don't confess negative things. Your words have power. Words, Words, Words. We've been hearing it and hearing it all the days of our Christian lives!!

The irony of my ministry is the fact that I teach people things that they already know. They just may not have connected the dots yet.

Words are seeds. They will produce exactly what they describe, or say, or intend. Just as a small seed will produce a 75 foot Oak tree, your words will produce your dream home. You bought it when you asked for it and received it when you prayed. Without money, and without price. When the time comes for the manifestation, the money will be there waiting for you.

How does God do it? By confirming the Word.... with signs following.

Okay, in a previous message I mentioned, "preventive maintenance," and "pay it forward" with those ideas in your thinking, let's see how God thinks.

Gen. 18:21
I will go down now, and see whether they have done altogether according to the cry of it, which is come unto me; and if not, I will know.

God, thinking in advance, said, when I get there, "I will know."

Let's say you're kicking along in life as normal and one day you decide, I want my own house and without a mortgage. So, according to the knowledge you have acquired about the Kingdom of God, you ask God for a house and that it come paid for. Then you go on about your business EXPECTING, until the house manifests.

Jas. 1:17
Every good gift and every perfect gift is from above, and cometh down from the Father of lights, with whom is no variableness, neither shadow of turning.

This thing is clearly outside the realm of your control, you're barely making it now as it is. The request didn't cost you a dime. Instead of saying "paying" it forward, let's say "calling" it forward. OR, let's use a more Biblical term, calling those things that be not as though they were.

How's that for clarity?

What do you want? Speak it, doubt not in your heart, but believe for it, it'll come!

Mk. 4:26-29
26. And he said, So is the kingdom of God, as if a man should cast seed into the ground;
27. And should sleep, and rise night and day, and the seed should spring and grow up, he knoweth not how.
28. For the earth bringeth forth fruit of herself; first the blade, then the ear, after that the full corn in the ear.
29. But when the fruit is brought forth, immediately he putteth in the sickle, because the harvest is come.

There's so much prepared for us, will we ever understand it all? The Word says that He will spend the ages revealing things to us.

We must learn to live our lives by our words. If you say, 3:00pm. Bust the door at 3:00!! Be there!! People are counting on you!! If a person's word is no good, the person is no good!! Mean what you say, and say what you mean. It's more important than you can imagine in this natural world.

The true riches…are Words!! Words spoken, with the intent, that they will actually happen.

Lk. 12:32
Fear not, little flock; for it is your Father's good pleasure to give you the kingdom.

● ● ● ●

Day - 4
"The Keys of the Kingdom"
(Matthew 16:19)

Kingdom Seekers
WEEK 4 DAY 4
01-09-2014

The keys of the Kingdom? In a word, "promises." The promises of God are His direct will for His people.

1 Jo. 5:14-15
14. And this is the confidence that we have in him, that, if we ask any thing according to his will, he heareth us:
15. And if we know that he hear us, whatsoever we ask, we know that we have the petitions that we desired of him.

Enough said? This kinda reminds me of the teachings of Jesus on unforgiveness, and judgmentalism.

▶ Unforgiveness:
Mt. 6:14-15
14. For if ye forgive men their trespasses, your heavenly Father will also forgive you:
15. But if ye forgive not men their trespasses, neither will your Father forgive your trespasses.

Mk. 11:25-26
25. And when ye stand praying, forgive, if ye have ought against any: that your Father also which is in heaven may forgive you your trespasses.
26. But if ye do not forgive, neither will your Father which is in heaven forgive your trespasses.

▶ Judgmentalism:
Mt. 7:1-2
1. Judge not, that ye be not judged.
2. For with what judgment ye judge, ye shall be judged: and with what measure ye mete, it shall be measured to you again.

Lk. 6:37
Judge not, and ye shall not be judged: condemn not, and ye shall not be condemned: forgive, and ye shall be forgiven:

Simple, so very simple. There's no need for further explanation. The promises are God's will for His people.

Mt. 8:17
That it might be fulfilled which was spoken by Esaias the prophet, saying, Himself took our infirmities, and bare our sicknesses.

That promise is designed to effect healing for anyone who will confess it, doubt not in their heart, but believe what they said shall come to pass.

Isn't that what Jesus said?

Mt. 21:21-22
21. Jesus answered and said unto them, Verily I say unto you, If ye have faith, and doubt not, ye shall not only do this which is done to the fig tree, but also if ye shall say unto this mountain, Be thou removed, and be thou cast into the sea; it shall be done.
22. And all things, whatsoever ye shall ask in prayer, believing, ye shall receive.

Mk. 11:22-24
22. And Jesus answering saith unto them, Have faith in God.
23. For verily I say unto you, That whosoever shall say unto this mountain, Be thou removed, and be thou cast into the sea; and shall not doubt in his heart, but shall believe that those things which he saith shall come to pass; he shall have whatsoever he saith.
24. Therefore I say unto you, What things soever ye desire, when ye pray, believe that ye receive them, and ye shall have them.

Oh yeah, that IS what Jesus said!!

Who or what are you following, the doctrine of your denomination, or the sayings of Jesus?

Jo. 15:7
If ye abide in me, and my words abide in you, ye shall ask what ye will, and it shall be done unto you.

There's no gray area here in these statements. So I'll ask you again, who are you following, your denomination or Jesus? Your denominational teachings are limited, with Jesus' teachings, all things are possible.

Psa. 91 is cram-packed full of promises:
Psa. 91:1-16
1. He that dwelleth in the secret place of the most High shall abide under the shadow of the Almighty.
2. I will say of the LORD, He is my refuge and my fortress: my God; in him will I trust.

3. Surely he shall deliver thee from the snare of the fowler, and from the noisome pestilence.

4. He shall cover thee with his feathers, and under his wings shalt thou trust: his truth shall be thy shield and buckler.

5. Thou shalt not be afraid for the terror by night; nor for the arrow that flieth by day;

6. Nor for the pestilence that walketh in darkness; nor for the destruction that wasteth at noonday.

7. A thousand shall fall at thy side, and ten thousand at thy right hand; but it shall not come nigh thee.

8. Only with thine eyes shalt thou behold and see the reward of the wicked.

9. Because thou hast made the LORD, which is my refuge, even the most High, thy habitation;

10. There shall no evil befall thee, neither shall any plague come nigh thy dwelling.

11. For he shall give his angels charge over thee, to keep thee in all thy ways.

12. They shall bear thee up in their hands, lest thou dash thy foot against a stone.

13. Thou shalt tread upon the lion and adder: the young lion and the dragon shalt thou trample under feet.

14. Because he hath set his love upon me, therefore will I deliver him: I will set him on high, because he hath known my name.

15. He shall call upon me, and I will answer him: I will be with him in trouble; I will deliver him, and honour him.

16. With long life will I satisfy him, and show him my salvation.

(v.1) He that dwelleth in the secret place of the most High shall abide under the shadow of the Almighty. That's safety!!

(v.3) Surely he shall deliver thee from the snare of the fowler, and from the noisome pestilence. That's deliverance!!

(v.4b) ...his truth shall be thy shield and buckler.

What did Jesus say about God's truth? It shall "make" us free!! Make, denotes a process.

(v.5) Thou shalt not be afraid for the terror by night; nor for the arrow that flieth by day; That's confidence and security!!

(v.6) Nor for the pestilence that walketh in darkness; nor for the destruction that wasteth at noonday. Again, security!!

(v.7) A thousand shall fall at thy side, and ten thousand at thy right hand; but it shall not come nigh thee. More confidence and security!!

(v.8) Only with thine eyes shalt thou behold and see the reward of the wicked. That's peace that passes all understanding!!

(v.9, 10) There shall no evil befall thee, neither shall any plague come nigh thy dwelling.

That's protection!!

(v.11, 12) They shall bear thee up in their hands, lest thou dash thy foot against a stone.
That's favor and protection!!

(v.14) Because he hath set his love upon me, therefore will I deliver him...
That's deliverance and protection!!

(v.15) He shall call upon me, and I will answer him: I will be with him in trouble; I will deliver him, and honour him. Favor and Honor.

(v.16) With long life will I satisfy him, and show him my salvation.
We have already seen His salvation!!

Ro. 10:10
For with the heart man believeth unto righteousness; and with the mouth confession is made unto salvation.

...and with the "mouth" confession is made unto "salvation."

• **Mouth:** Okay, we're talking words again, being the only rate of exchange in the Kingdom of God.

• **Salvation:** The Greek word (soteria) *so-tay-ree-ah,* rescue or safety, deliver, health, salvation, save, saving.

Ro. 10:6-8
6. But the righteousness which is of faith speaketh on this wise, Say not in thine heart, Who shall ascend into heaven? (that is, to bring Christ down from above:)
7. Or, Who shall descend into the deep? (that is, to bring up Christ again from the dead.)
8. But what saith it? The word is nigh thee, even in thy mouth, and in thy heart: that is, the word of faith, which we preach;

Remember Paul's thorn?

2 Co. 12:8-10
8. For this thing I besought the Lord thrice, that it might depart from me.
9. And he said unto me, My grace is sufficient for thee: for my strength is made perfect in weakness. Most gladly therefore will I rather glory in my infirmities, that the power of Christ may rest upon me.
10. Therefore I take pleasure in infirmities, in reproaches, in necessities, in persecutions, in distresses for Christ' sake: for when I am weak, then am I strong.

Whether something has just happened to you, or you got yourself into a mess, you have God's Word, His Spirit, and His Name. Righteousness speaks!! You get yourself out of this mess by using the word of Faith which is able to save your soul from distress.

Jo. 14:13-14
13. And whatsoever ye shall ask in my name, that will I do, that the Father may be glorified in the Son.
14. If ye shall ask any thing in my name, I will do it.

How many ways do we have to see it, before we use it? Use what? The Word!!

Lk. 12:32
Fear not, little flock; for it is your Father's good pleasure to give you the kingdom.

●●●●●

Day - 5
"Discerner of Thoughts & Intents"
(Hebrews 4:12)

Kingdom Seekers
WEEK 4 DAY 5
01-10-2014

A couple of days ago while talking to another minister, the statement was made, I just don't understand what you're trying to say here by separating Jesus, from the Word, because Jesus is the Word!!

Correct, but, in this study we are not talking about Jesus in the Old Testament, we're talking about the Word. Jesus didn't come along until Mathew, Mark, Luke, and John, of the New Testament. Another way to say this is, we're talking about who Jesus was before He was Jesus.

Jesus had a beginning just like you and I did. The Word, however, always was and always will be. The object of this study is not Jesus, but The Word of God, before the Word was made flesh, and became the man Jesus.

I'll admit that it took me about three weeks to get comfortable with the idea of separating Jesus from the Word. What helped me was this:

Heb. 6:1-3
1. Therefore leaving the principles of the doctrine of Christ, let us go on unto perfection; not laying again the foundation of repentance from dead works, and of faith toward God,
2. Of the doctrine of baptisms, and of laying on of hands, and of resurrection of the dead, and

of eternal judgment.
3. And this will we do, if God permit.

Therefore leaving the principles of the doctrine of Christ, let us go on unto perfection. Can you imagine that? Leaving the principles of the doctrine of Christ?

Where did that come from?

I'll tell you where it came from, The Word of God, Hebrews 6:1-3!!! Take your eyes off Jesus for a moment and put them directly on the Word. It was the Word, in the OT that did everything.

Jo. 1:1-3
1. In the beginning was the Word, and the Word was with God, and the Word was God.
2. The same was in the beginning with God.
3. All things were made by him; and without him was not any thing made that was made.

It's all about the Word, in the OT, not the man Jesus. Take your eyes off Jesus for a moment and consider who, or maybe I should say "what," he really is, He is the Word of God!!

Jo. 14:13-14
13. And whatsoever ye shall ask in my name, that will I do, that the Father may be glorified in the Son.
14. If ye shall ask any thing in my name, I will do it.

The Word, is the "doer" of words spoken. The Word, produces or manifests what is spoken.

Jo. 14:21
He that hath my commandments, and keepeth them, he it is that loveth me: and he that loveth me shall be loved of my Father, and I will love him, and will manifest myself to him.

How do you think Jesus will manifest Himself? A personal visitation?

I don't think so. He will manifest Himself by confirming the Word, with signs following. IF YOU'RE BELIEVING FOR HIM TO!! IF NOT…HE'S NOT OBLIGATED TO DO ANYTHING. WITHOUT FAITH, IT IS IMPOSSIBLE TO PLEASE GOD!!

Check this out.
Heb. 1:1-3
1. God, who at sundry times and in divers manners spake in time past unto the fathers by the prophets,
2. Hath in these last days spoken unto us by his Son, whom he hath appointed heir of all things, by whom also he made the worlds;
3. Who being the brightness of his glory, and the express image of his person, and upholding all

things by the word of his power, when he had by himself purged our sins, sat down on the right hand of the Majesty on high;

Did you catch it?

Upholding all things by the word of his power. God has placed the power to produce in what is said....in the words themselves!! God doesn't have to lift a finger, He has placed His almighty power in words, as seeds able to produce what is said in Faith.

We must learn to speak with purpose and intent, expecting what we say will definitely happen. That's where our words will definitely pass the acid test.

Jo. 1:14
And the Word was made flesh, and dwelt among us, (and we beheld his glory, the glory as of the only begotten of the Father,) full of grace and truth.

NOW, we have Jesus!! The Word of God in person. Listen....the Word, (deity) and (the man Jesus,) did not merge, or blend, or come together until the resurrection.

Why? Because He had to overcome the devil as a man, not as deity.

The devil overcame man and took the dominion that God gave man on the earth. Jesus had to do everything He did, as a man, not deity, in order to make things right. The man Jesus didn't have anything more going for Him then, than you do today.

You are His body on the earth today. You have His Word, His Spirit, and His Name. if God be for you, who can be against you? All things are possible to him that believeth!!

Yeah but, I don't have the money, or I don't have the equipment, or means to do this!! Hey, that's ok, you have Words!! An unlimited supply. Go ahead and call those things that be not as though they were. What do you want? Describe it... with your words.

God said, and it was so. God said, and it was so. And God saw that it was good. in other words, God said something, the Word, performed the doing of what God said, and God saw that it was done right!!

Which brings us to today's message.

Heb. 4:12
For the word of God is quick, and powerful, and sharper than any twoedged sword, piercing even to the dividing asunder of soul and spirit, and of the joints and marrow, "and is a discerner of the thoughts and intents of the heart."

"and is a discerner of the thoughts and intents of the heart."

Now that Jesus' humanity and deity are merged together, we need to understand that when we received Jesus as saviour, the Word of God came into our hearts. The same Word that God released in Genesis, now lives in us.

Righteousness speaks!! Dictate policy in your life! The Word will confirm it. Confirm what? WHAT-YOU-SAID!!

Do you want to walk in divine health? Start talking about it, frame it with words, expecting, until it comes to pass in your life.

He is in you!! He knows….He knows if you're believing for it or not. He knows if you're just saying it because the Bible says it. You can't fool Him. He knows!! He knows what you're thinking, and He knows what you intend to do when you get what you're believing for.

Grow up!!!! in the knowledge of Him. Are we using God by using the Word? Don't be stupid!!

He put these truths in His Word to bless us and provide for us an abundant life.

1 Jo. 5:13-15
13. These things have I written unto you that believe on the name of the Son of God; that ye may know that ye have eternal life, and that ye may believe on the name of the Son of God.
14. And this is the confidence that we have in him, that, if we ask any thing according to his will, he heareth us:
15. And if we know that he hear us, whatsoever we ask, we know that we have the petitions that we desired of him.

Jo. 14:13-14
13. And whatsoever ye shall ask in my name, that will I do, that the Father may be glorified in the Son.
14. If ye shall ask any thing in my name, I WILL DO IT.

Now don't be asking God to help you in your drug business, or to have that couple down the street divorce so that you can marry the spouse. You can't get God involved in your sin.

Think, before you ask. Is your request spiritual, made in righteousness and true holiness, or is it carnal, made according to the lust of the flesh?

The flesh never says…enough!

It was the Word, on salvation that produced salvation. It will be the Word, on healing that will produce healing. Yes, the Word, now has a name, His name is Jesus, but don't take your mind off the fact that He is the Word of God.

All things were created by Him, and for Him, and by Him do all things consist. He is the Word of God's power.

Col. 1:13
Who hath delivered us from the power of darkness, and hath translated us into the kingdom of his dear Son:

2 Pet. 1:11
For so an entrance shall be ministered unto you abundantly into the everlasting kingdom of our Lord and Saviour Jesus Christ.

Lk. 12:32
Fear not, little flock; for it is your Father's good pleasure to give you the kingdom.

■ ◻ ■ ◻ ■

Week-5
God's Thoughts and Ways

Week-5-Days-1-5
God's Thoughts and Ways:
Day-1. And God Said, and it Was So. Gen. 1:1-26
Day-2. So shall My Word Be. Isa. 55:8-11
Day-3. Promises, Truths and Spiritual Laws. Gen. 11:1-9
Day-4. Mighty Through God. 2 Co. 10:4-5
Day-5. Entering God's Rest. Heb. 4:1-11

●

Day - 1
"And God Said, and it Was So"
(Genesis 1:1-26)

Kingdom Seekers
WEEK 5 DAY 1
01-13-2014

Gen. 1:3-4a
3. "And God said," Let there be light: and there was light.
4. And "God saw the light, that it was good"...

Gen. 1:9-10b
9. "And God said," Let the waters under the heaven be gathered together unto one place, and let the dry land appear:and it was so.

(v.10) ...and God saw that it was good.

Gen. 1:11-12
11. "And God said," Let the earth bring forth grass, the herb yielding seed, and the fruit tree yielding fruit after his kind, whose seed is in itself, upon the earth: and it was so.
12. And the earth brought forth grass, and herb yielding seed after his kind, and the tree yielding fruit, whose seed was in itself, after his kind: "and God saw that it was good."

Gen. 1:14
"And God said," Let there be lights in the firmament of the heaven to divide the day from the night; and let them be for signs, and for seasons, and for days, and years:

Gen. 1:18
And to rule over the day and over the night, and to divide the light from the darkness: and God saw that it was good.

Gen. 1:20-21
20. "And God said," Let the waters bring forth abundantly the moving creature that hath life, and fowl that may fly above the earth in the open firmament of heaven.
21. And God created great whales, and every living creature that moveth, which the waters brought forth abundantly, after their kind, and every winged fowl after his kind: "and God saw that it was good."

Gen. 1:24-25
24. "And God said," Let the earth bring forth the living creature after his kind, cattle, and creeping thing, and beast of the earth after his kind: "and it was so."
25. And God made the beast of the earth after his kind, and cattle after their kind, and every thing that creepeth upon the earth after his kind: "and God saw that it was good."

Gen. 1:26-27
26. "And God said," Let us make man in our image, after our likeness: and let them have dominion over the fish of the sea, and over the fowl of the air, and over the cattle, and over all the earth, and over every creeping thing that creepeth upon the earth.
27. So God created man in his own image, in the image of God created he him; male and female created he them.

Gen. 1:29-30
29. "And God said," Behold, I have given you every herb bearing seed, which is upon the face of all the earth, and every tree, in the which is the fruit of a tree yielding seed; to you it shall be for meat.
30. And to every beast of the earth, and to every fowl of the air, and to every thing that creepeth upon the earth, wherein there is life, I have given every green herb for meat: "and it was so."

Gen. 1:31
"And God saw every thing that he had made, and, behold, it was very good." And the evening and the morning were the sixth day.

Okay, every time we see "And God said," we need to understand that God doesn't have any tools. He doesn't have a road grader, or chainsaw, or a cordless drill. When God wants to do something, He uses Words to describe what He wants done…then the Words go out and perform the doing of what God said.

For the purpose of this study, let's rephrase that last statement. (When God wants to do something, He uses Words to describe what He wants done…then the "WORD" goes out and performs the doing of what God said.

We're focusing on the "Word of God" here. Not the Bible per say, but the second part of the God-head of the OT, The Father, the Word, and The Holy Spirit. The Word is a sentient being, the second person of the Godhead. Today we see Him as The Father, The Son, and The Holy Spirit, because in,

Jo. 1:14
And the Word was made flesh, and dwelt among us, (and we beheld his glory, the glory as of the only begotten of the Father,) full of grace and truth.

Now….The Word, has a name, we call Him Jesus. Jesus, is the Word!!

Everytime we see " and it was so," we need to understand that after God said it, the Word went out and did it. "And it was so," the Word went out and performed the doing of what God said.

Okay…let's bring that over into NT teaching and terminology. *(Mk. 16:20)* "And Jesus, confirmed the Word, with signs following!!"

LIGHT BE, LIGHT WAS!! The Word went out and created the sun with all it's attributes, just far enough, but not too far, from the earth. Because The Word knew what God intended.

NOTE: God didn't have to go into detail about the sun's attributes, the Word, which was in Him, and He knew what God was thinking and what God intended, and just went on out there and did it!!

My point is this…..In your prayer time, you don't have to be so nit-pickin persnickety descriptive about your request. The Word is in you. He knows what you want and how you want it. He knows how many you want right down to the color you want it to be.

And that's why…everytime you see "and God saw that it was good," it means, THE WORD…DID IT…RIGHT!! The Word, confirmed God's words, with signs following.

Prv. 8:1-36
1. Doth not wisdom cry? and understanding put forth her voice?
2. She standeth in the top of high places, by the way in the places of the paths.
3. She crieth at the gates, at the entry of the city, at the coming in at the doors.
4. Unto you, O men, I call; and my voice is to the sons of man.
5. O ye simple, understand wisdom: and, ye fools, be ye of an understanding heart.
6. Hear; for I will speak of excellent things; and the opening of my lips shall be right things.
7. For my mouth shall speak truth; and wickedness is an abomination to my lips.
8. All the words of my mouth are in righteousness; there is nothing froward or perverse in them.

9. *They are all plain to him that understandeth, and right to them that find knowledge.*

10. *Receive my instruction, and not silver; and knowledge rather than choice gold.*

11. *For wisdom is better than rubies; and all the things that may be desired are not to be compared to it.*

12. *I wisdom dwell with prudence, and find out knowledge of witty inventions.*

13. *The fear of the LORD is to hate evil: pride, and arrogancy, and the evil way, and the froward mouth, do I hate.*

14. *Counsel is mine, and sound wisdom: I am understanding; I have strength.*

15. *By me kings reign, and princes decree justice.*

16. *By me princes rule, and nobles, even all the judges of the earth.*

17. *I love them that love me; and those that seek me early shall find me.*

18. *Riches and honour are with me; yea, durable riches and righteousness.*

19. *My fruit is better than gold, yea, than fine gold; and my revenue than choice silver.*

20. *I lead in the way of righteousness, in the midst of the paths of judgment:*

21. *That I may cause those that love me to inherit substance; and I will fill their treasures.*

22. *The LORD possessed me in the beginning of his way, before his works of old.*

23. *I was set up from everlasting, from the beginning, or ever the earth was.*

24. *When there were no depths, I was brought forth; when there were no fountains abounding with water.*

25. *Before the mountains were settled, before the hills was I brought forth:*

26. *While as yet he had not made the earth, nor the fields, nor the highest part of the dust of the world.*

27. *When he prepared the heavens, I was there: when he set a compass upon the face of the depth:*

28. *When he established the clouds above: when he strengthened the fountains of the deep:*

29. *When he gave to the sea his decree, that the waters should not pass his commandment: when he appointed the foundations of the earth:*

30. *Then I was by him, as one brought up with him: and I was daily his delight, rejoicing always before him;*

31. *Rejoicing in the habitable part of his earth; and my delights were with the sons of men.*

32. *Now therefore hearken unto me, O ye children: for blessed are they that keep my ways.*

33. *Hear instruction, and be wise, and refuse it not.*

34. *Blessed is the man that heareth me, watching daily at my gates, waiting at the posts of my doors.*

35. *For whoso findeth me findeth life, and shall obtain favour of the LORD.*

36. *But he that sinneth against me wrongeth his own soul: all they that hate me love death.*

Jesus is made unto us Knowledge, Wisdom, and Understanding.

●●

Day - 2
"So shall My Word Be"
(Isaiah 55:8-11)

Kingdom Seekers
WEEK 5 DAY 2
01-14-2014

Isa. 55:8-11
8. For my thoughts are not your thoughts, neither are your ways my ways, saith the LORD.
9. For as the heavens are higher than the earth, so are my ways higher than your ways, and my thoughts than your thoughts.
10. For as the rain cometh down, and the snow from heaven, and returneth not thither, but watereth the earth, and maketh it bring forth and bud, that it may give seed to the sower, and bread to the eater:
11. So shall my word be that goeth forth out of my mouth: it shall not return unto me void, but it shall accomplish that which I please, and it shall prosper in the thing whereto I sent it.

God's thoughts are higher than our thoughts. God sees the whole picture. He knows what's going to happen.

Though our insights are limited, God has given us promises that by these, like God, we can see the end from the beginning of our circumstances.

Can we learn how to think the way God thinks? Certainly!! If it weren't for the promises… maybe not, but we do have promises from God.

Jesus put it this way, I am the Way, the Truth, and the Life.

By whose stripes we were healed is designed to affect a healing for us. The power to produce that healing is in the words themselves. God has placed His power in His Word, He doesn't even have to lift a finger, He just speaks, and what He says, comes to pass.

Can we learn to do that?

Daaaahhh…yes. We are created in His image and after His likeness. Plus, we have been given some exceeding great and precious promises that by these we have been invited to be partakers of the divine nature. So, in verse 8 we see that God sees things differently. He sees the end from the beginning, the whole picture.

Can we do that?

Yes! Through the promises, we too can see the end from the beginning of our circumstances.

Next….we see that God's ways are different than our ways. If we want to remove a tree, we will need a chainsaw and maybe a stump grinder to do the job right. God, on the other hand merely speaks to the tree, and it removes to yonder place.

Can we do things God's way?

At first…no. but as we grow in the knowledge of God and His Kingdom, YES, we can.

Jo. 14:14-15
14. And this is the confidence that we have in him, that, if we ask any thing according to his will, he heareth us:
15. And if we know that he hear us, whatsoever we ask, we know that we have the petitions that we desired of him.

Jo. 14:13-14
13. And whatsoever ye shall ask in my name, that will I do, that the Father may be glorified in the Son.
14. If ye shall ask any thing in my name, I will do it.

I can't help but wonder, what part of "whatsoever" we don't understand?

Mt. 21:21-22
21. Jesus answered and said unto them, Verily I say unto you, If ye have faith, and doubt not, ye shall not only do this which is done to the fig tree, but also if ye shall say unto this mountain, Be thou removed, and be thou cast into the sea; it shall be done.
22. And all things, whatsoever ye shall ask in prayer, believing, ye shall receive.

Mk. 11:23-24
23. For verily I say unto you, That whosoever shall say unto this mountain, Be thou removed, and be thou cast into the sea; and shall not doubt in his heart, but shall believe that those things which he saith shall come to pass; he shall have whatsoever he saith.
24. Therefore I say unto you, What things soever ye desire, when ye pray, believe that ye receive them, and ye shall have them.

Lk. 17:6
And the Lord said, If ye had faith as a grain of mustard seed, ye might say unto this sycamine tree, Be thou plucked up by the root, and be thou planted in the sea; and it should obey you.

Jo. 15:7
If ye abide in me, and my words abide in you, ye shall ask what ye will, and it shall be done unto you.

YES…we can do this!! God has given us a way.

Jesus put it this way, I am the Way, the Truth, and the Life.

Next, we have verse *10*.
For as the rain cometh down, and the snow from heaven, and returneth not thither, but watereth the earth, and maketh it bring forth and bud, that it may give seed to the sower, and bread to the eater:

Rain doesn't fall on the earth just to evaporate and return to the atmosphere. It waters the earth that it may bring forth and bud, giving seed to the sower and bread to the eater. Rain's job description, is to produce a harvest of something.

Every seed will produce after it's own kind. (every promise of God will produce after its own kind)

Enough said? No….apparently not, so let's continue.

(v.11) So shall my word be that goeth forth out of my mouth: it shall not return unto me void, but it shall accomplish that which I please, and it shall prosper in the thing whereto I sent it.

God likens His Word to water in this verse. So shall My Word be… God's Word comes down, but it doesn't water the earth, it waters the hearts of men. We are God's husbandry. He waters and sows, His Word into our hearts, that IT may bring forth and bud, For the earth bringeth forth fruit of herself; first the blade, then the ear, after that the full corn in the ear.

God's Word will not return to Him void, dysfunctional, empty, or non-productive.

Only love and faith filled words will reach God.

God's Word shall accomplish that thing which He pleases, and God's Word shall prosper in the thing whereto He sent it.

So…what's my point? When God's Word leaves OUR mouths, it shall accomplish that which God pleases in our lives, and it shall prosper in the thing whereto WE sent it!!

The angels of God hearken to the voice of God on the earth.

Heb. 1:13-14
13. But to which of the angels said he at any time, Sit on my right hand, until I make thine enemies thy footstool?

14. Are they not all ministering spirits, sent forth to minister for them who shall be heirs of salvation?

When we speak God's Word on the earth, the angels recognize the Word of the Lord, and go into action so that when the time of harvest comes, everything will be ready for us when we get there.

Isa. 55:10 is like Mk. 11:23.

Isa. 55:10
For as the rain cometh down, and the snow from heaven, and returneth not thither, but watereth the earth, and maketh it bring forth and bud, that it may give seed to the sower, and bread to the eater:

Mk. 11:23
For verily I say unto you, That whosoever shall say unto this mountain, Be thou removed, and be thou cast into the sea; and shall not doubt in his heart, but shall believe that those things which he saith shall come to pass; he shall have whatsoever he saith.

Isa. 55:11 is like Mk. 11:24.

Isa. 55:11
So shall my word be that goeth forth out of my mouth: it shall not return unto me void, but it shall accomplish that which I please, and it shall prosper in the thing whereto I sent it.

Mk. 11:24
Therefore I say unto you, What things soever ye desire, when ye pray, believe that ye receive them, and ye shall have them.

Jo. 14:21
He that hath my commandments, and keepeth them, he it is that loveth me: and he that loveth me shall be loved of my Father, and I will love him, and will manifest myself to him.

How would Jesus manifest himself to us? A personal visitation?

I don't think so. I know Him, and I know His ways. He will manifest Himself most likely by confirming the Word, with signs following. It's part of His job description, it's what He does, but hey, He might give you a personal visitation…cool!

Jo. 16:23-24
23. And in that day ye shall ask me nothing. Verily, verily, I say unto you, Whatsoever ye shall ask the Father in my name, he will give it you.
24. Hitherto have ye asked nothing in my name: ask, and ye shall receive, that your joy may be full.

In that day… Simple prayer instruction for the church age, TO THE FATHER, IN JESUS NAME!!

Mt. 7:7-8
7. Ask, and it shall be given you; seek, and ye shall find; knock, and it shall be opened unto you:
8. For every one that asketh receiveth; and he that seeketh findeth; and to
him that knocketh it shall be opened.

Lk. 12:32
Fear not, little flock; for it is your Father's good pleasure to give you the kingdom.

● ● ●

Day - 3
"Promises, Truths & Spiritual Laws"
(Genesis 11:1-9)

Kingdom Seekers
WEEK 5 DAY 3
01-15-2014

Gen. 11:1-9
1. And the whole earth was of one language, and of one speech.
2. And it came to pass, as they journeyed from the east, that they found a plain in the land of Shinar; and they dwelt there.
3. And they said one to another, Go to, let us make brick, and burn them thoroughly. And they had brick for stone, and slime had they for mortar.
4. And they said, Go to, let us build us a city and a tower, whose top may reach unto heaven; and let us make us a name, lest we be scattered abroad upon the face of the whole earth.
5. And the LORD came down to see the city and the tower, which the children of men builded.
6. And the LORD said, Behold, the people is one, and they have all one language; and this they begin to do: and now nothing will be restrained from them, which they have imagined to do.
7. Go to, let us go down, and there confound their language, that they may not understand one another's speech.
8. So the LORD scattered them abroad from thence upon the face of all the earth: and they left off to build the city.
9. Therefore is the name of it called Babel; because the LORD did there confound the language of all the earth: and from thence did the LORD scatter them abroad upon the face of all the earth.

Okay, though I haven't said this in this study yet, I need to point out that I say things that the Bible simply does-not-say. For instance, the Bible does not say that a spirit will never cease to exist. However, the Bible does speak of eternal separation from God, which is known as spiritual, or the second death.

Natural death is nonexistence, the natural body goes back to the dust of the earth and no longer exists.

However, once a spirit is created, it will never cease to exist. It undergoes what is called, the second death, which is eternal separation from God. Eternal punishment, and torment. So we can say that a spirit will never die, as we know death, but will live, or exist, apart from God, and be aware of it's surroundings forever.

(v.6) And the LORD said, Behold, the people is one, and they have all one language; and this they begin to do: and now nothing will be restrained from them, which they have imagined to do.

What we need to see in vrs 6 is this, *and now nothing will be restrained from them, which they have imagined to do.*

Mk. 11:23 was already in place, Mt. 18:19 must have already been in place.

God's Word is from eternity past, present, and future. God's Word is not subject to change, not even a shadow of turning. Spiritual Law was in effect in Genesis, as well as now!!

(v.7) Go to, let us go down, and there confound their language, that they may not understand one another's speech.

God had to go down to confound their language so that they could no longer agree. Spiritual law was, is, and will continue to work forever, every time we put it to work!! It will never fail!!

Do you remember the lesson of Week-4-Days-1-5? Exact Knowledge, knowledge that is so focused, so exact it qualifies to be a truth. Yet, it is so true, so exact, so focused, it qualifies to be a law, and that's not even all.

God's knowledge is designed to produce itself, or bring itself to pass. WOW, that's power!! Outrageous in its buying power, and dynamic in its working. The true riches.

We have all the wealth we will ever need because it comes in the form of Words, not cash. "Outrageous in its buying power" because it doesn't matter whether you're buying a box of tooth picks, or a multi-million dollar ministry headquarters. We buy without money, and without price.

You might ask, how did you get that Ram Charger in '86? I received it at the prayer meeting four months earlier. When the time came for the harvest, the money was there waiting for me.

"Dynamic in its working" because words can change a diseased heart into a brand new heart.

Can you buy a new one? Sure, but at what cost, $100,000 or so?

In The KINGDOM of GOD we can buy it without money, and without price, and without going under the knife.

Find a promise that covers your need, speak it, doubt not in your heart, but believe what you said shall come to pass. God is not lying, or fooling around here. What things soever ye desire, when ye pray, believe that ye receive them, and ye shall have them PERIOD!!

Put the promise to work, put the truth to work for you. God's Word is Law, established forever. It will work every time you put it to work. Here's another way of saying that, once you learn how the system works, WORK-THE-SYSTEM!!

Jesus said, My words, they are spirit and they are life.

Question: When are your words going to be spirit and life? What are you saying about your circumstances?

Are you saying what the world has taught you? It's no use, we just can't make it. The flu season is here, I'll be the first one in the family to get it. The lay-off is next month, I'll be the first one out the door.

Or, are you saying what God has taught you? *I can do all things through Christ that strengthens me. No weapon formed against me shall prosper. No plague shall come nigh my dwelling, and whatsoever I do shall prosper. Nothing by any means, shall hurt me.*

God has given us a free will. Like Moses, God has set before us, life and death, blessing, and cursing, chose ye therefore life and blessing.

No man has been dragged into the knowledge of The KINGDOM kicking and screaming. No man has casually sauntered into the knowledge of The KINGDOM by accident. You must press in, the violent, energetic, take it by force.

You must be teachable.

Lk. 18:17
Verily I say unto you, Whosoever shall not receive the kingdom of God as a little child shall in no wise enter therein.

A child believes every thing that mommy and daddy says.

Read your own Bible. See what God is saying to you.

Mk. 4:21-25
21. And he said unto them, Is a candle brought to be put under a bushel, or under a bed? and not to be set on a candlestick?
22. For there is nothing hid, which shall not be manifested; neither was any thing kept secret, but that it should come abroad.
23. If any man have ears to hear, let him hear.
24. And he said unto them, Take heed what ye hear: with what measure ye mete, it shall be measured to you: and unto you that hear shall more be given.
25. For he that hath, to him shall be given: and he that hath not, from him shall be taken even that which he hath.

Why did He say, from him shall be taken even that which he hath?

Simple,
(v.15) And these are they by the way side, where the word is sown; but when they have heard, Satan cometh immediately, and taketh away the word that was sown in their hearts.

You know, the Bible says in
2 Co. 4:3-4
3. But if our gospel be hid, it is hid to them that are lost:
4. In whom the god of this world hath blinded the minds of them which believe not, lest the light of the glorious gospel of Christ, who is the image of God, should shine unto them.

That means that before you received Jesus as saviour, your mind was blinded too.

The Bible clearly states,
Eph. 4:23-24
23. And be renewed in the spirit of your mind;
24. And that ye put on the new man, which after God is created in righteousness and true holiness.

Col. 3:9-10
9. Lie not one to another, seeing that ye have put off the old man with his deeds;
10. And have put on the new man, which is renewed in knowledge after the image of him that created him:

Ro. 12:2
And be not conformed to this world: but be ye transformed by the renewing of your mind, that ye may prove what is that good, and acceptable, and perfect, will of God.

Renewing of the mind is not automatic. That's something that God has told us to do, and it won't get done until YOU DO IT!! From what, to what? From the world's thoughts and ways, to God's thoughts and ways!! How's that for a start? Jesus didn't have any thing more going for Him than we do right now. We have His Name, His Word, and His Spirit.

If God be for us, who can be against us?

Lk. 12:32
Fear not, little flock; for it is your Father's good pleasure to give you the kingdom.

●●●●

Day - 4
"Mighty Through God"
(II Corinthians 10:4-5)

Kingdom Seekers
WEEK 5 DAY 4
01-16-2014

2 Co. 10:3-5
3. For though we walk in the flesh, we do not war after the flesh:
4. (For the weapons of our warfare are not carnal, but mighty through God to the pulling down of strong holds;)
5. Casting down imaginations, and every high thing that exalteth itself against the knowledge of God, and bringing into captivity every thought to the obedience of Christ;

We can see here that guns and knives will serve us no good in the good fight of faith. Even a court injunction, though it is handed down on paper,…in words,…is not a weapon for spiritual dealings.

Listen to this,
Prv. 4:20-23
20. My son, attend to my words; incline thine ear unto my sayings.
21. Let them not depart from thine eyes; keep them in the midst of thine heart.
22. For they are life unto those that find them, and health to all their flesh.
23. Keep thy heart with all diligence; for out of it are the issues of life.

Keep thy heart,…the inner man, the hidden man of the heart and the knowledge that you have acquired. If carnal knowledge comes out your mouth, you're sunk. You've lost the battle.

However, if spiritual knowledge comes out your mouth, you will be able to overcome all circumstances. All things are possible to him that believes.

What did Jesus say about the heart?

Mk. 11:23
…and shall not doubt in his heart, but shall believe…

Lk. 6:45

A good man out of the good treasure of his heart bringeth forth that which is good; and an evil man out of the evil treasure of his heart bringeth forth that which is evil: for of the abundance of the heart his mouth speaketh.

Lk. 12:34

For where your treasure is, there will your heart be also. For of the abundance of the heart his mouth speaketh.

Got it? Enough said?

It's words only in The KINGDOM of GOD, use them wisely. With your words, you can bind yourself up in bitter bondage, or set yourself free. It's not God's "place," it's your "call."

What are you saying about your circumstances? Are you planting good seed for future needs?

Do you want a house, and have it come paid for?

Start talking about it now, frame it with words, even if you don't see how God will do it. Go ahead and call those things that be not, as though they were. In due time, the house will come.

Why?

Mk. 4:26-29

26. So is the kingdom of God, as if a man should cast seed into the ground;

27. And should sleep, and rise night and day, and the seed should spring and grow up, he knoweth not how.

28. For the earth bringeth forth fruit of herself; first the blade, then the ear, after that the full corn in the ear.

29. But when the fruit is brought forth, immediately he putteth in the sickle, because the harvest is come.

For the earth bringeth forth fruit of herself…. In case you don't remember what the earth is…it is the hearts of men!! God sows His Word into your heart, and out of your heart comes forth the fruit of the Word.

What do you need?

What do you want?

Speak it, doubt not in your heart, but believe what you said shall come to pass.

Isn't that what Jesus said?

Who are you following? Some man standing in a pulpit? ...or His Majesty, the King of Eternity?

No weapon formed against you shall prosper!!

How about the doctor's report, the bank's policy, or the city fathers that won't let you build that garage on your property where you want it. The doctors, banks, and city fathers are not your problem. It's principalities, powers, and rulers of darkness in high places, THAT'S YOUR PROBLEM!!

Speak to them, drive them out of your affairs.

Can you do that?

Yes, yes, yes, yes, yes, you can do that!! If, you know who you are in Christ.

If you don't, they'll bowl you over and beat you down.

1 Pet. 5:6-11
6. Humble yourselves therefore under the mighty hand of God, that he may exalt you in due time:
7. Casting all your care upon him; for he careth for you.
8. Be sober, be vigilant; because your adversary the devil, as a roaring lion, walketh about, seeking whom he may devour:
9. Whom resist stedfast in the faith, knowing that the same afflictions are accomplished in your brethren that are in the world.
10. But the God of all grace, who hath called us unto his eternal glory by Christ Jesus, after that ye have suffered a while, make you perfect, stablish, strengthen, settle you.
11. To him be glory and dominion for ever and ever. Amen.

Heb. 4:12-13
12. For the word of God is quick, and powerful, and sharper than any twoedged sword, piercing even to the dividing asunder of soul and spirit, and of the joints and marrow, and is a discerner of the thoughts and intents of the heart.
13. Neither is there any creature that is not manifest in his sight: but all things are naked and opened unto the eyes of him with whom we have to do.

The Word, Jesus is in you. Put Him to work on your behalf. You're not abusing Him, or His generosity.

He flat out told us,
Jo. 14:13-14
13. And whatsoever ye shall ask in my name, that will I do, that the Father may be glorified in the Son.
14. If ye shall ask any thing in my name, I will do it.

Like my wife says to the person in front of us at a traffic signal ...WHAT COLOR OF GREEN ARE YOU WAITING FOR!! Speak, doubt not, but believe!!

The same Word that God released in Genesis, is now in you. ...and the seed should spring and grow up, he knoweth not how. Praise God we don't have to understand it, just do it!! It'll work, every time we put it to work.

It, the Word, is mighty through God to the pulling down of strongholds. Casting down imaginations and every high thing that exalts itself against the knowledge of God. Bringing into captivity, every thought, to the obedience of Christ, (or as we would say it in this study) bringing into captivity, every thought to the obedience of the Word!!

Because that's who Christ is, The Word of God. You are limited to the Word of God, "the Bible," and your own imagination, as to what you can do on the earth in this lifetime. In case you haven't noticed, you are unlimited!! Not even to your imagination, because when we reach the outer boundary of our imagination, God reveals more to us.

I pray that you be filled with the knowledge of Him, and increasing in the knowledge of Him. How can one increase when he is full? More revelation, larger capacity.

Lk. 12:32
Fear not, little flock; for it is your Father's good pleasure to give you the kingdom.

●●●●●

Day - 5
"Entering God's Rest"
(Hebrews 4:1-11)

Kingdom Seekers
WEEK 5 DAY 5
01-17-2014

Heb. 4:1-12
1. Let us therefore fear, lest, a promise being left us of entering into his rest, any of you should seem to come short of it.
2. For unto us was the gospel preached, as well as unto them: but the word preached did not profit them, not being mixed with faith in them that heard it.
3. For we which have believed do enter into rest, as he said, As I have sworn in my wrath, if they shall enter into my rest: although the works were finished from the foundation of the world.
4. For he spake in a certain place of the seventh day on this wise, And God did rest the seventh day from all his works.

5. And in this place again, If they shall enter into my rest.

6. Seeing therefore it remaineth that some must enter therein, and they to whom it was first preached entered not in because of unbelief:

7. Again, he limiteth a certain day, saying in David, To day, after so long a time; as it is said, To day if ye will hear his voice, harden not your hearts.

8. For if Jesus had given them rest, then would he not afterward have spoken of another day.

9. There remaineth therefore a rest to the people of God.

10. For he that is entered into his rest, he also hath ceased from his own works, as God did from his.

11. Let us labour therefore to enter into that rest, lest any man fall after the same example of unbelief.

12. For the word of God is quick, and powerful, and sharper than any twoedged sword, piercing even to the dividing asunder of soul and spirit, and of the joints and marrow, and is a discerner of the thoughts and intents of the heart.

Today we are going to be looking at something that you "absolutely do not have to believe."

The Genesis account shows us that God rested on the seventh day, and we are taught that we should do the same.

Right? Well, I don't think that this is what Hebrews 4 is talking about. Also, I don't think that was what Jesus was saying in

Mt. 11:28-30
28. Come unto me, all ye that labour and are heavy laden, and I will give you rest.
29. Take my yoke upon you, and learn of me; for I am meek and lowly in heart: and ye shall find rest unto your souls.
30. For my yoke is easy, and my burden is light.

Pay particular attention to
Heb. 4:10
For he that is entered into his rest, he also hath ceased from his own works, as God did from his.

The Saturday, day of rest has changed to Sunday. When we make request of God, we are not taught just to wait till Saturday to receive our request. No, we're taught to make our request, doubt not in our hearts, but believe that we receive it even as we're praying, and then, it's on the way to us.

So, what's my point?

In Genesis, when God was saying all that He was saying, He rested from His sayings, EX-PECTING, until His Words came to pass.

The real point of entering into God's rest is this, when we have symptoms, we have the God given right to say, Himself took our infirmities, and bare our sicknesses, He forgives all my iniquities; and heals all my diseases, and by His stripes, I was healed!! When we do that, we open the door for healing to take place. We have put the Word out there, just like God did in Genesis, EXPECTING, until OUR Words come to pass!! At least that's how the system works.

If you work the system or not… remains to be seen. In The KINGDOM of GOD, we live by our words, and when we speak words of truth, expecting, we're going to get what we said. We are all in a receiving position with God. After we have prayed believing we received, now we're in a receiving posture….EXPECTING.

If you're not expecting, your not exercising Faith, and Jesus is not obligated to confirm our words with signs following.

We need to learn to direct our words as royalty. We need to learn to declare a thing, expecting that it become the law of the land in our realm of influence.

Drive the enemy out of our camp, and out of our affairs.

When we have said our peace, we should enter into the "God kind" of rest, expecting, till our words come to pass!! Is it as simple as that? Yes, it is as simple as that. When you have ceased from your own works, "sayings" go ahead and rest assured that your words are working, and will surely come to pass.

Do you remember what Jesus said, in
Mk. 4:18-19
18. And these are they which are sown among thorns; such as hear the word,
19. And the cares of this world, and the deceitfulness of riches, and the lusts of other things entering in, choke the word, and it becometh unfruitful.

When you get your mind off God's promise and get concerned about other things, you choke the Word, and it becomes unfruitful. That tells us that the Word WAS working, but we got off on some other tangent and the Word became unfruitful.

Jesus told us to be anxious for nothing!! Relax, we can take a lesson from the centurion, speak the Word only, and your needs will be met!!

Jesus, is in you. He knows if you're believing for that thing or not. If you're believing for it, you're going to get it! If you're not, well, you need to go back to the Bible, stir yourself up, and pray again.

The Word will work. Every time you put it to work. Use the Word. Apply the Word to your life situations, trials, and circumstances.

You're not abusing the Word, or God, He's there to help in time of need. Come boldly to the Throne of Grace, and plead your case, on the one hand, and on the other hand get in the face of the devil and drive him out of your affairs!! Resist him and he will flee from you.

(v.9) There remaineth therefore a rest to the people of God.

(v.10) For he that is entered into his rest, he also hath ceased from his own works, as God did from his.

Resting on Saturday is indeed a Biblical teaching, but I don't think that that's what Hebrews is pointing out.

Those things you want in life, start talking about them now, receive them now in your prayer time. It doesn't cost a dime. We buy, and otherwise acquire things, without money and without price.

What you have been freely given, give freely. That includes the Word of God, and that vacation home you don't use anymore. Or that motorcycle, or car, or desk, or whatever it is you have that you don't use or need anymore.

Come on think, where no money is, there is no greed!!

Yes there are times that you would sell something to finance a deal, but when you can, give freely, it didn't cost you anything!! Did it?

Get on the other side of this learning curve.

■ ◻ ■ ◻ ■ ◻

Week-6
Delivered From the Power of Darkness

Week-6-Days-1-5
Delivered From the Power of Darkness:
Day-1. Walk as Children of Light. Eph. 5:8
Day-2. Redeemed From the Curse of the Law. Gal. 3:13
Day-3. No More Tossed To and Fro. Eph. 4:13-14
Day-4. This is the Confidence. 1 Jo. 5:13-14
Day-5. The Perfect Law of Liberty. Jas. 1:25

●

Day - 1
"Walk as Children of Light"
(Ephesians 5:8)

Kingdom Seekers
WEEK 6 DAY 1
01-20-2014

Eph. 5:8
For ye were sometimes darkness, but now are ye light in the Lord: walk as children of light:

Col. 1:12-18
12. Giving thanks unto the Father, which hath made us meet to be partakers of the inheritance of the saints in light:
13. Who hath delivered us from the power of darkness, and hath translated us into the kingdom of his dear Son:
14. In whom we have redemption through his blood, even the forgiveness of sins:
15. Who is the image of the invisible God, the firstborn of every creature:
16. For by him were all things created, that are in heaven, and that are in earth, visible and invisible, whether they be thrones, or dominions, or principalities, or powers: all things were created by him, and for him:
17. And he is before all things, and by him all things consist.
18. And he is the head of the body, the church: who is the beginning, the firstborn from the dead; that in all things he might have the preeminence.

Do you remember a few lessons ago I mentioned preventive maintenance, and pay it forward?

I saw a TV episode last night that struck my attention. It wasn't the plot, but it was part of the story line. There were vets coming back from war zones with short term memory problems.

Today's subject is Walk as Children of Light. We have been delivered from the power of darkness and have been translated into The KINGDOM of GOD, where all things are possible.

This principle is not restricted to this profession, but I'll use this profession to bring out the point. Let's say you work in a hospital that deals with short term memory problems. If you were to begin to say "this day" Monday, 1-20-14, that every returning soldier I work with will be healed, and delivered from all mental problems, not at some point, but even as I am working with them.

Now there's a bold statement, impossible in the natural, but totally within the power of KINGDOM RULE. If you say these words with forethought, and intent, and doubt not in your heart that it will surely come to pass. And purpose in your heart that it will be, even as you have said, the Word that is in you, Jesus, will confirm that desire with signs following.

As I said, in the natural this is completely and utterly impossible, but in the Spirit, all things are possible.

Do you see where I'm going with this? Walk as children of light!!

Mt. 5:16
Let your light so shine before men, that they may see your good works, and glorify your Father which is in heaven.

We are open epistles before men. God gave me this illustration a few years ago. The Bible says that Israel is God's jewel, they were supposed to show forth God, to all nations but they didn't. They kept Him to themselves.

What does a jewel do when light hits it? It sends out beams of light, like a lighthouse that warns ships of impending danger.

The Church however, is likened to a pearl.

What does a pearl do when light hits it? It absorbs light.

The light of the church is more like a street light. It's light only shines out for several yards. The illustration is this, a lighthouse shoots out beams of light showing the way. A street light only shows light for a short distance. Though a person is standing ten miles away, he or she can see the light. They are still in outer darkness, but they can see the light.

1 Co. 13:12
For now we see through a glass, darkly; but then face to face: now I know in part; but then shall I know even as also I am known.

Let your light so shine. There's a commercial on TV right now that states that the natural eye can see a candle light from ten miles away.

Prv. 20:27
The spirit of man is the candle of the LORD, searching all the inward parts of the belly. Again I say, let your light so shine.

1 Tim. 4:15
Meditate upon these things; give thyself wholly to them; that thy profiting may appear to all.

Psa. 1:1-3
1. Blessed is the man that walketh not in the counsel of the ungodly, nor standeth in the way of sinners, nor sitteth in the seat of the scornful.
2. But his delight is in the law of the LORD; and in his law doth he meditate day and night.
3. And he shall be like a tree planted by the rivers of water, that bringeth forth his fruit in his season; his leaf also shall not wither; and whatsoever he doeth shall prosper.

You are like a tree planted by the rivers of water, that brings forth fruit in your season!! Trees don't bear fruit for themselves …they bear fruit for others ….many others!!

Walk as Children of Light. Let others see your profiting and good works.

We used a doctor's or nurse's role in this principle of preventive maintenance, and pay it forward illustration. It doesn't matter what your field of endeavor is. Whether your profession is house painting, or carpentry, or a CPA accountant.

What do you want? Frame it with words. Doubt not in your heart, but believe it will be even as you said.

Jo. 14:13-14
13. And whatsoever ye shall ask in my name, that will I do, that the Father may be glorified in the Son.
14. If ye shall ask any thing in my name, I WILL DO IT.

Unprecedented success is at your fingertips. If you only knew it, you would be walking in the blessing of it right now!!

The devil has already blinded your mind to the things of God.

We must renew our minds to the things of God, his Son, His Spirit, and His KINGDOM. Get on the other side of this learning curve of life. Start ruling in life with Jesus, and stop speculating and surmising and just trying to make the best of a bad situation like the world does.

Jesus, "The Word," said, I am the Way, the Truth, and the Life. Take control of your life, learn who you are in Jesus.

Put a pair of animals in a valley for a hundred years and all you will have is a bunch of animals.

But put a man and a woman in a valley for a hundred years and you will have homes, and towns. Railroads, and eighteen wheelers, I-pads and cell phones. We are creative beings. Even un-born-again people. We are all creative people.

The closest men have ever got to the faith message is "the power of positive thinking." They don't know how it works, but they just know it works.

You are not on the outside looking in. You are in The KINGDOM of GOD.

Mt. 11:29-30
29. Take my yoke upon you, and learn of me; for I am meek and lowly in heart: and ye shall find rest unto your souls.
30. For my yoke is easy, and my burden is light.

Lk. 12:32
Fear not, little flock; for it is your Father's good pleasure to give you the kingdom.

You now, are the light.

●●
Day - 2
"Redeemed From the Curse of the Law"
(Galatians 3:13)

Kingdom Seekers
WEEK 6 DAY 2
01-21-2014

Gal. 3:13-14
13. Christ hath redeemed us from the curse of the law, being made a curse for us: for it is written, Cursed is every one that hangeth on a tree:
14. That the blessing of Abraham might come on the Gentiles through Jesus Christ; that we might receive the promise of the Spirit through faith.

Most of us already know that the curse of the law consists of three principle things, Poverty, Sickness, and Death.

Concerning the issues of life, when you boil it on down, what we have are three things. Life, health, and wealth. All other issues fade by comparison.

What could be more important than life itself? I'm speaking of course as a born-again Christian.

In having life, what could be more important than having the wherewithal (financially) to enjoy that life, and help others to enjoy life? Having a prosperous life wouldn't have much benefit if one was sick all the time, so health is also very important.

There are entire denominations of Christians, people who love God, but are stupid enough to think that God uses sickness as a tool to teach them something. Stupid, Stupid, Stupid!!! It is a tool alright, of the devil to prove that God lied, when He said "Himself took our infirmities and bear our sickness, and by His stripes, we were healed." YEA, HATH GOD NOT SAID?

That's the game he plays. He cannot attack God directly, so he attacks God through us. If one doesn't resist by submitting themselves to God and His Word, but receives the symptoms as from God, who are we to blame God, or the man?

God may use the situation to teach you something, but God didn't put that on you. The devil did and you bought it with the words of your own mouth. Stupid!!

God has made a way out for you by His Word,

Psa. 103:3
He forgives all our iniquities and heals all our sicknesses,

Mt. 8:17
Himself took our infirmities, and bare our sicknesses,

1 Pet. 2:24
...by whose stripes ye were healed.

2 Tim. 2:25
In meekness instructing those that oppose themselves; if God peradventure will give them repentance to the acknowledging of the truth;

How does one oppose himself? By his words, or how he thinks? OR BOTH!!

Part of my ministry is to change the way people think, if I can change the way you think, YOU will change the way YOU speak.

God's promises are His will for His people!!

I used to have a problem with believing that it was God's will for me. I mean ME.

So He asked me one day, "Are you in Christ?"

"Yes Lord."

Then the promise is to you, individually…collectively.

Hey folks, He has set a table for us in the presence of our enemies. Divine health is on the table. Receive it the same way you received salvation.

You heard the Word on salvation, you doubted not in your heart, but believed it, and you said with your mouth….Lord Save Me.

Ro. 10:10
For with the heart man believeth unto righteousness; and with the mouth confession is made unto…

(Whatever you're believing for, salvation, healing, prosperity, protection, deliverance, peace of mind, a college education for your kids, a safe dependable car for your family, success in your business, the healing of your estranged family, getting that horse your daughter is wanting so desperately, come on….think, what do you want in life?)

Jo. 10:10
The thief cometh not, but for to steal, and to kill, and to destroy: I am come that they might have life, and that they might have it more abundantly.

God doesn't mind if you have things. Cars, trucks, motorcycles hang-gliders, 60 inch TVs, or whatever. He just doesn't want those things to possess you.

Where no money is involved, there is no greed. If you bought the hang-glider at the prayer meeting, without money and without price, why wouldn't you give it to someone who wants, or needs it when God inspires you to give it away?

1 Co. 2:9-12
9. But as it is written, Eye hath not seen, nor ear heard, neither have entered into the heart of man, the things which God hath prepared for them that love him.
10. But God hath revealed them unto us by his Spirit: for the Spirit searcheth all things, yea, the deep things of God.
11. For what man knoweth the things of a man, save the spirit of man which is in him? even so the things of God knoweth no man, but the Spirit of God.
12. Now we have received, not the spirit of the world, but the spirit which is of God; that we

might know the things that are freely given to us of God.

God has made a way for us to live life according to KINGDOM RULE, on planet earth.

Mk. 4:21-25
21. And he said unto them, Is a candle brought to be put under a bushel, or under a bed? and not to be set on a candlestick?
22. For there is nothing hid, which shall not be manifested; neither was any thing kept secret, but that it should come abroad.
23. If any man have ears to hear, let him hear.
24. And he said unto them, Take heed what ye hear: with what measure ye mete, it shall be measured to you: and unto you that hear shall more be given.
25. For he that hath, to him shall be given: and he that hath not, from him shall be taken even that which he hath.

We are redeemed from poverty, sickness, and death.

Walk as children of light. Conduct yourself as God sees you, not as you see you!! God, has made a way for us to live an abundant life, if you can hear it, you can walk in it.

How does a man oppose himself? By the words of his own mouth!!

Renew your mind to the things of God. This is not a journey into The KINGDOM of GOD, you were born here, it is a journey into the "knowledge" of The KINGDOM of GOD.

Do you remember what was said about the lighthouse and the street light on the corner in the last lesson?

You were born in righteousness and true holiness, but you are out there in outer darkness, if you see the light, move toward it.

Eph. 5:14
Wherefore he saith, Awake thou that sleepest, and arise from the dead, and Christ shall give thee light. (insight, understanding.)

Prv. 4:5-8
5. Get wisdom, get understanding: forget it not; neither decline from the words of my mouth.
6. Forsake her not, and she shall preserve thee: love her, and she shall keep thee.
7. Wisdom is the principal thing; therefore get wisdom: and with all thy getting get understanding.
8. Exalt her, and she shall promote thee: she shall bring thee to honour, when thou dost embrace her.

● ● ●

Day - 3
"No More Tossed To and Fro"
(Ephesians 4:13-14)

Kingdom Seekers
WEEK 6 DAY 3
01-22-2014

Eph. 4:13-15
13. Till we all come in the unity of the faith, and of the knowledge of the Son of God, unto a perfect man, unto the measure of the stature of the fulness of Christ:
14. That we henceforth be no more children, tossed to and fro, and carried about with every wind of doctrine, by the sleight of men, and cunning craftiness, whereby they lie in wait to deceive;
15. But speaking the truth in love, may grow up into him in all things, which is the head, even Christ:

I am an obscure preacher. Publicly speaking, no one knows my name. I have no reputation to protect, and to be honest, I kind of enjoy my anonymity. I don't have to answer to a lot of people for the things I teach and preach. I am ordained with a ministry that I do answer to, but they stand behind me in whatever I teach....so far! lol.

When I was sitting in the congregation, I didn't realize that the man in the pulpit could be wrong.

We are all a product of what we've been taught. It was only after I stood in the pulpit after studying for my own messages that I realized that the Bible doesn't really say what I've been told it says.

You will notice it too, if you'll ever read your own Bible.

What changed me was the fact that I am a disciple. The Bible is talking to me, and for the first time, I am hearing!!

Mk. 4:21-25
21. And he said unto them, Is a candle brought to be put under a bushel, or under a bed? and not to be set on a candlestick?
22. For there is nothing hid, which shall not be manifested; neither was any thing kept secret, but that it should come abroad.
23. If any man have ears to hear, let him hear.
24. And he said unto them, Take heed what ye hear: with what measure ye mete, it shall be measured to you: and unto you that hear shall more be given.
25. For he that hath, to him shall be given: and he that hath not, from him shall be taken even that which he hath.

Don't be deceived by every wind of doctrine. Check everything out in your own Bible. See what it is saying to you.

I recently tried to share this Bible study course with a certain denominational church. The pastor asked me if I had documents to show what I would be teaching. I gave him a copy of the study course which unfortunately had a copy of the study overview.

I point that out because the whole study course is scripture only, no personal notes, no comments, just scripture.

It was the overview that alarmed him. It showed all the titles and subtitles. The same ones you've been seeing, (Dead to sin, The Mind of Christ, Righteousness Speaks, The Disciple & the Servant, The Weapons of our Warfare, Leaving the Principles and Doctrine of Christ, The True Riches, The Keys of The KINGDOM, And God said, and it was so, Entering God's Rest, Delivered from the Power of Darkness, Redeemed from the Curse of the Law, No More Tossed To and Fro.

I have recently included in the study, "The Perfect Law of Liberty." Now there's one I'll bet you have never heard before, not in any church that I've ever heard of.

It'll set many folks free from the bondage of self condemnation, and misery. Stay Tuned!!

The minister told me that he thought the study would be a conflict of interest, and I couldn't teach it in his church.

WHAT??? It is 100% scripture….and he said…it was a conflict of interest. WOW!

You know, in the great by-n-by, we're all going to be on the same page, but as for the here and now….buyer beware!!

If you think sickness is God's way of teaching you something, well, we're all a product of what we've been taught. God may use the sickness to teach you something, but He didn't put the sickness on you!! That's stupid!!

That's a lie right out of the pit of hell.

YEA, HATH GOD NOT SAID? It's the same ol, same ol game that the devil plays.

Do you remember the movie "Jeremiah Johnson?" the mountain man told the tenderfoot, "everything you learned down on the flat will serve you no good up here."

I'm telling you straight out, everything you learned in this natural realm will serve you no good in The KINGDOM of GOD!!! You cannot compare natural experience, with spiritual power and truth.

There is a host of translations of the Bible. Personally, I use the King James Version, what I call "the real Bible." All other translations are aimed at the carnal mind of reason so people can "try" to understand what they're reading.

Truth be known, your not going to understand unless the Spirit of God, which is in you, reveals it to you. We live in a closed society, you can't get to the Father, except by the Son. You can't see the Son, except the Father reveals Him to you. The Bible, may as well be still in the original Greek and Hebrew.

Like Jesus said, the violent take it by force. You must want it with all your heart. You must press in!!

Men are born in the Kingdom, but they don't know anything about the Kingdom. They are in outer darkness, and unless they come to the Light, they will stay in outer darkness, SAVED, but ignorant of the things of God. His Son, His Spirit, and His Kingdom.

Read your own Bible!! What is Jesus saying to YOU. Yeah but, His words are only in Red.

No!! In this study, we're talking about the Word. We left the principles and doctrine of Christ. The Bible from Genesis to Revelation is The Word of God. All of it? Yes…all of it!!

Haven't you made the distinction between the OT Word, and the NT Jesus yet?

We're talking about the Word, in this study, not Jesus the man.

I know it's hard, it took me some weeks to make the distinction but it is necessary to understand how the Word, works. It was the Word on salvation that saved you. It will be the Word on healing that will heal you. It will be the Word on protection that will protect you. It's the Word, it's the Word, it's the Word, it's the Word that will be confirmed with signs following!!!!

Don't be deceived, and don't deceive yourself.

Eph. 4:14
That we henceforth be no more children, tossed to and fro, and carried about with every wind of doctrine, by the sleight of men, and cunning craftiness, whereby they lie in wait to deceive;

Jas. 1:21-22
21. Wherefore lay apart all filthiness and superfluity of naughtiness, and receive with meekness the engrafted word, which is able to save your souls.
22. But be ye doers of the word, and not hearers only, deceiving your own selves.

Lk. 12:32
Fear not, little flock; for it is your Father's good pleasure to give you the kingdom.

••••

Day - 4
"This is the Confidence"
(I John 5:13-14)

Kingdom Seekers
WEEK 6 DAY 4
01-23-2014

1 Jo. 5:14-15
14. And this is the confidence that we have in him, that, if we ask any thing according to his will, he heareth us:
15. And if we know that he hear us, whatsoever we ask, we know that we have the petitions that we desired of him.

What could be more simple than this? Asking God, for things that we know, are God's will for us!!

As we have seen previously in this study, the promises are God's will for His people. The promises are to Abraham's seed. If you're in Jesus, you are Abraham's seed. The promises are to you, individually and collectively.

We can ask for healing, because we know, He forgives all our iniquities and heals all our diseases, Himself took our infirmities, and bare our sicknesses and by His stripes, we were healed. We can ask for prosperity, because we know that we are like trees planted by the rivers of water, that brings forth our fruit in our season, and our leaf shall not wither, and whatsoever we do shall prosper.

I don't care if all you want to do, is sell green gravel to men that don't want to mow their yards!! Your business will prosper!!

Why? Because of the Word!!

Remember now, we're not looking at Jesus just now, we're looking at the Word,…which was… who Jesus was… before it was Jesus. In the OT "It/He" was the Word!!

In the NT "It/He" became flesh, and we now call "It/He" Jesus of Nazareth, the Christ, Who performed the doing of redemption, and salvation. He now stands at the ready, ready to confirm with signs following, whatever promise we are believing for today.

I know I keep hammering you on this, but we must understand, Jesus was the Word, before He was Jesus, and it's the Word on the promise that will produce what the promise says, or describes.

Jo. 14:21
He that hath my commandments, and keepeth them, he it is that loveth me: and he that loveth me shall be loved of my Father, and I will love him, and will manifest myself to him.

How do you think Jesus is going to manifest Himself to someone?

By a personal appearance?

I don't think so. I believe He will manifest Himself by confirming the Word with signs following. Jesus is the Word, He is designed to produce whatever is said… by God…or man!!

Jo. 14:13-14
13. And whatsoever ye shall ask in my name, that will I do, that the Father may be glorified in the Son.
14. If ye shall ask any thing in my name, I WILL DO IT.

The written Word, on paper, is not designed to produce itself.

It is the Rhema, "the spoken Word," there's where the power lies. When we speak, the Word, it produces what was said. God said, and it was so. God said, and it was so. God said, and it was so.

Fred said, and it was so. Johnny said, and it was so. Albert, Shirley, and Joyce said, and it was so.

It's as a man should cast a seed in the ground and should sleep and rise night and day, and the seed should grow up, we know not how…but we do know…every seed produces after it's own kind. The Word is designed to produce itself with signs following.

Come on church, let's get on the other side of this learning curve. Go ahead and call those things that be not, as though they were…hide and watch… and just see if what you said comes to pass!!

The Word…Jesus is in you. He is a discerner of the thoughts and intents of the heart. He knows if you're believing "for" what you said…or not. If you're believing "for it" He's going to produce for you. If you're not believing "for it" He's not obligated to confirm that saying for you. Enough said??

Let me repeat,
Jo. 14:13-14
13. And whatsoever ye shall ask in my name, that will I do, that the Father may be glorified in the Son.
14. If ye shall ask any thing in my name, I WILL DO IT.

The devil has our minds blinded to the truth of the WORD OF GOD!!

Listen to this,
Isa. 55:8-11
8. For my thoughts are not your thoughts, neither are your ways my ways, saith the LORD.

9. For as the heavens are higher than the earth, so are my ways higher than your ways, and my thoughts than your thoughts.

10. For as the rain cometh down, and the snow from heaven, and returneth not thither, but watereth the earth, and maketh it bring forth and bud, that it may give seed to the sower, and bread to the eater:

11. So shall my word be that goeth forth out of my mouth: it shall not return unto me void, but it shall accomplish that which I please, and it shall prosper in the thing whereto I sent it.

As the rain comes down and waters the earth that it bring forth and bud. God's Word comes down and waters our "heart" that it brings forth and buds giving seed for the sower and bread for the eater.

Without words, The KINGDOM of GOD would be dysfunctional. It wouldn't work. His Kingdom is based on the seed, plant, harvest principle. His Word will not return to Him void, ineffective, or dysfunctional.

Find a promise that covers your need, speak it, doubt not in your heart, but believe what you said shall come to pass. Isn't that what Jesus said so many times?

Mt. 17:20
If ye have faith as a grain of mustard seed, ye shall say unto this mountain, Remove hence to yonder place; and it shall remove; and nothing shall be impossible unto you.

Mt. 21:22
And all things, whatsoever ye shall ask in prayer, believing, ye shall receive.

Mk. 11:24
Therefore I say unto you, What things soever ye desire, when ye pray, believe that ye receive them, and ye shall have them.

Lk. 17:6
And the Lord said, If ye had faith as a grain of mustard seed, ye might say unto this sycamine tree, Be thou plucked up by the root, and be thou planted in the sea; and it should obey you.

Jo. 14:13-14
13. And whatsoever ye shall ask in my name, that will I do, that the Father may be glorified in the Son.

14. If ye shall ask any thing in my name, I will do it.

Jo. 15:7
If ye abide in me, and my words abide in you, ye shall ask what ye will, and it shall be done unto you.

Jo. 16:24
Hitherto have ye asked nothing in my name: ask, and ye shall receive, that your joy may be full.

Is your confidence still in what you have learned in the world?

You still need to renew your mind to the way God thinks, and the way God does things. He speaks, and what He says, comes to pass. You are created in God's image and after His likeness. You are a creative being!! Create a life that you're comfortable with!! Enough said?

Lk. 12:32
Fear not, little flock; for it is your Father's good pleasure to give you the kingdom.

●●●●●

Day - 5
"The Perfect Law of Liberty"
(James 1:25)

Kingdom Seekers
WEEK 6 DAY 5
01-24-2014

Jas. 1:22-25
22. But be ye doers of the word, and not hearers only, deceiving your own selves.
23. For if any be a hearer of the word, and not a doer, he is like unto a man beholding his natural face in a glass:
24. For he beholdeth himself, and goeth his way, and straightway forgetteth what manner of man he was.
25. But whoso looketh into the perfect law of liberty, and continueth therein, he being not a forgetful hearer, but a doer of the work, this man shall be blessed in his deed.

When have you ever heard this explained? No church I've ever been to.

Most people who hear the message on Grace, say, you're just giving us a license to sin!!

Well…you poor thing…men are sinning without a license, didn't you know that? Besides that, who do you think you are that God, would give you a license to sin? He is not giving out licenses, He has done something about it.

Ro. 5:19-21

19. For as by one man's disobedience many were made sinners, so by the obedience of one shall many be made righteous.

20. Moreover the law entered, that the offence might abound. But where sin abounded, grace did much more abound:

21. That as sin hath reigned unto death, even so might grace reign through righteousness unto eternal life by Jesus Christ our Lord.

I have determined to keep these writings limited to one page on my documents format on my computer. So, you're going to have some home-work today.

In order to understand the law of liberty, you need to read, Ro. 5:1-21. Where we will see, verses: *(v.1) Therefore being justified by faith, we have peace with God through our Lord Jesus Christ: (v.8) But God commendeth his love toward us, in that, while we were yet sinners, Christ died for us. (v.10) For if, when we were enemies, we were reconciled to God by the death of his Son, much more, being reconciled, we shall be saved by his life. (v.19) For as by one man's disobedience many were made sinners, so by the obedience of one shall many be made righteous. (v.20) Moreover the law entered, that the offence might abound. But where sin abounded, grace did much more abound:*

We are justified by Faith in Jesus' work of redemption, while we were yet sinners, Christ died for us. When we were still enemies, we were reconciled to God by the death of His Son, where sin abounded, grace did much more abound.

Next, read Ro. 6:1-23. Where we will see, verses: *(v.2) God forbid. How shall we, that are dead to sin, live any longer therein? (v.7) For he that is dead is freed from sin. (v.11) Likewise reckon ye also yourselves to be dead indeed unto sin, but alive unto God through Jesus Christ our Lord. (v.14) For sin shall not have dominion over you: for ye are not under the law, but under grace. (v.15) What then? shall we sin, because we are not under the law, but under grace? God forbid. (v.18) Being then made free from sin, ye became the servants of righteousness. (v.20) For when ye were the servants of sin, ye were free from righteousness. (v.23) For the wages of sin is death; but the gift of God is eternal life through Jesus Christ our Lord.*

We are dead to sin, freed from sin, alive unto God, we are not under law, but under grace, we are servants of righteousness. (Born in Righteousness and true Holiness)

Then read Ro. 7:1-25. there's a lot of good stuff in Ro. 7. But I'm running out of space, so I'll point out verses

(v.24) O wretched man that I am! who shall deliver me from the body of this death?

(v.25) I thank God through Jesus Christ our Lord. So then with the mind I myself serve the law of God; but with the flesh the law of sin.

What about the sin we still do and so easily besets us?

Okay,

Ro. 8:1-3

1. There is therefore now no condemnation to them which are in Christ Jesus, who walk not after the flesh, but after the Spirit.

2. For the law of the Spirit of life in Christ Jesus hath made me free from the law of sin and death.

3. For what the law could not do, in that it was weak through the flesh, God sending his own Son in the likeness of sinful flesh, and for sin, condemned sin in the flesh:

God condemned sin in the flesh so that sin could no longer lord it over us and condemn us... God condemned "it!!"

1 Jo. 3:5-9

5. And ye know that he was manifested to take away our sins; and in him is no sin.

6. Whosoever abideth in him sinneth not: whosoever sinneth hath not seen him, neither known him.

7. Little children, let no man deceive you: he that doeth righteousness is righteous, even as he is righteous.

8. He that committeth sin is of the devil; for the devil sinneth from the beginning. For this purpose the Son of God was manifested, that he might destroy the works of the devil.

9. Whosoever is born of God doth not commit sin; for his seed remaineth in him: and he cannot sin, because he is born of God.

We do not sin, because we cannot sin, because we are born of God!!

Ro. 14:22

Hast thou faith? have it to thyself before God. Happy is he that condemneth not himself in that thing which he alloweth.

Let me ask you a question. Do you think God is behind child molesters, murders, robbers and thieves? No, of course not!!

When you did that sin, you allowed yourself to do that. It was no longer you that do it, but sin that dwells in you.

You are washed, you are clean. You are born of God. YOU-SIN-NOT!! Where no law is, there is no transgression. You are in Jesus. Your righteousness is of Him, not your own.

Men say, I was a sinner but now I'm saved by grace!

The Bible says, while we were yet sinners, Christ died for us. The flesh carries the sin nature. The spirit carries the righteousness nature.

Was 1 Jo. 1:9 written for us to feel better, or for God to feel better?

I think it was written for us because God, has taken care of everything. We, on our own, can do nothing to make it better or worse. It's out of our hands!

Just like in the creation account, God made man… last!! And saw that every thing that He had made was very good.

When you do sin, pick yourself up, dust yourself off, and keep on truckin, because your Father has already done something about it, ALL that needs to be done about it!!

It's no longer you, but sin that dwells in you that's doing that stuff. He knows your heart, He knows you don't want to do that anymore.

Lk. 12:32
Fear not, little flock; for it is your Father's good pleasure to give you the kingdom.

You will be REIGNITED, ENCOURAGED and BUILT-UP IN YOUR FAITH as Missionary Pastor & Author Daryl P Holloman shares his inspired MASTERWORK

"Daryl has a calling to empower the Body of Christ with powerful teaching and preaching of God's Word."
-- David Barber
Missionary/Evangelist

"Like pages from The Book of Acts, being friends with Daryl Holloman is an adventure. A true Christ-like example of Love, Joy, Faith and Patience."
-- Aaron Jones
Revivalist and Artist

"I just love Jesus, Brother. That's all, I just love Jesus!"
-- Daryl P Holloman
Missionary Pastor & Author

6"x9" over 500 pages
ISBN 13: 978-0-9904376-1-1
Copyright © 2014 Daryl P Holloman

Seemed Good to
THE HOLY GHOST
Five Anointed Teachings by Brother Daryl

PLUS PRAYERS, PROPHECY TESTIMONIES and more...

Available now at select Bookstores and
www.BoldTruthPublishing.com

■ □ ■ □ ■ □ ■

Week-7
Gifts and Fruit of the Spirit

Week-7-Days-1-5
Gifts and Fruit of the Spirit:
Day 1. The Ministry Gifts. Eph. 4:11
Day 2. Gifts & Fruit of the Spirit. 1 Co. 12:1-11, Gal. 5:22
Day 3. The Perfecting of the Saints. Eph. 4:12-16
Day-4. The Stature of the Fullness of Christ. Eph. 4:13
Day-5. Tithes and Offerings. Mal. 3:7-12

●

Day - 1
"The Ministry Gifts"
(Ephesians 4:11)

Kingdom Seekers
WEEK 7 DAY 1
01-27-2014

Eph. 4:11-13
11. And he gave some, apostles; and some, prophets; and some, evangelists; and some, pastors and teachers;
12. For the perfecting of the saints, for the work of the ministry, for the edifying of the body of Christ:
13. Till we all come in the unity of the faith, and of the knowledge of the Son of God, unto a perfect man, unto the measure of the stature of the fulness of Christ:

The Apostle, Prophet, Evangelist, Pastor, and Teacher. We call them the five fold ministry gifts.

What's their job?

● **#1. The perfecting of the saints.**

You know what, I don't think that hammering people about their natural human behavior is perfecting anything. What that does, it causes people to take their eyes off Jesus, and puts them directly on themselves. That leads people into self-righteousness, negating the finished work of

Jesus. It will also cause people to fall from grace and go back under the law of Moses.

The curse of the law is still out there. Self-righteousness will kill you.

Col. 2:20-22
20. Wherefore if ye be dead with Christ from the rudiments of the world, why, as though living in the world, are ye subject to ordinances,
21. (Touch not; taste not; handle not;
22. Which all are to perish with the using;) after the commandments and doctrines of men?

Teaching that we are dead to sin, and that we should live no longer in it, will bring a person to spiritual maturity a lot easier than hammering somebody about their behavior. Because his behavior is a continuing situation.

Ro. 7:14-17
14. For we know that the law is spiritual: but I am carnal, sold under sin.
15. For that which I do I allow not: for what I would, that do I not; but what I hate, that do I.
16. If then I do that which I would not, I consent unto the law that it is good.
17. Now then it is no more I that do it, but sin that dwelleth in me.

Ro. 7:25
I thank God through Jesus Christ our Lord. So then with the mind I myself serve the law of God; but with the flesh the law of sin.

Now that's the truth of the Word of God. What is your pastor teaching?

● **#2. For the work of the ministry.**

Ro. 11:29
For the gifts and calling of God are without repentance.

God is not sorry that He called you, and gave you gifts. The gifts and callings stand. Whether you ever walk in them, or not. We all have gifts, we all have callings, but God will not force us to use them against our will.

When Jesus was here, He had all the gifts without measure. The body of Christ, on the earth has all the gifts, but no one man has all the gifts like Jesus did.

Did you notice that? God determines who gets the gifts, and what gifts they get. If you don't know what your gift is, join the club!!

I thank God that I now know what my gift is, and that I walk in it.

Though the body has all the gifts, we may not walk in them all the time. If we need the gift of "the word of wisdom," or "the discerning of spirits" I believe it will be available to us, though we may not walk in the "office" of that gift all the time.

All God needs is that someone in authority on the earth, to stand in the gap and intercede on behalf of the need, in order for God to move in on the scene with His mighty power to minister to the needs of the people.

Remember the Centurion in Lk. 7:2-10? *(v.8) For I also am a man set under authority, having under me soldiers, and I say unto one, Go, and he goeth; and to another, Come, and he cometh; and to my servant, Do this, and he doeth it.*

We are under authority on the earth. God given authority. In an earthly kingdom, the people serve the king, in taxes and lands, pomp and circumstance.

In The KINGDOM of GOD, God serves the people. He meets our needs, gives us the desires of our hearts, and makes sure that our joy is full. He takes care of us, and we minister to Him in the form of praise and worship for who He is and what He's done.

I mentioned a tree bearing fruit the other day. A tree does not bear fruit for itself.

Your gifts are for the people you minister to in the body of Christ, and to those whom you minister to outside the body. Your gifts and calling are without repentance.

Do you have to walk in them?

No. are you still saved?

Yes. To whom much is given, much will be required. If you have not received anything more than salvation, not much will be required of you.

Are you catching the inference?

You can be a spiritual giant on the earth, if you set your heart to it, but it's not required of you.

Only those who press in, will enter, into the knowledge of The KINGDOM. Use what you have. Walk as children of light according to knowledge, not speculation. There's no guessing about what God will do. He has shown us how He thinks, how He does things, and what His will is through His promises. Go ahead and act like this is all second nature to you because it is, you have been born again, in Him.

You were alive in God once, before the foundation of the world, but you died. That's why we need to "re"-new our minds to the things of God.

Eph. 1:4
According as he hath chosen us in him before the foundation of the world, that we should be holy and without blame before him in love

What love is that?

The love described in
1 Co. 13:4-7
4. Charity suffereth long, and is kind; charity envieth not; charity vaunteth not itself, is not puffed up,
5. Doth not behave itself unseemly, seeketh not her own, is not easily provoked, thinketh no evil;
6. Rejoiceth not in iniquity, but rejoiceth in the truth;
7. Beareth all things, believeth all things, hopeth all things, endureth all things.

Hey, another insight on the Perfect law of Liberty….no extra charge!

●●

Day - 2
"Gifts & Fruit of the Spirit"
(I Corinthians 12:1-11, Galatians 5:22)

Kingdom Seekers
WEEK 7 DAY 2
01-28-2014

1 Co. 12:1-11
1. Now concerning spiritual gifts, brethren, I would not have you ignorant.
2. Ye know that ye were Gentiles, carried away unto these dumb idols, even as ye were led.
3. Wherefore I give you to understand, that no man speaking by the Spirit of God calleth Jesus accursed: and that no man can say that Jesus is the Lord, but by the Holy Ghost.
4. Now there are diversities of gifts, but the same Spirit.
5. And there are differences of administrations, but the same Lord.
6. And there are diversities of operations, but it is the same God which worketh all in all.
7. But the manifestation of the Spirit is given to every man to profit withal.
8. For to one is given by the Spirit the word of wisdom; to another the word of knowledge by the same Spirit;
9. To another faith by the same Spirit; to another the gifts of healing by the same Spirit;
10. To another the working of miracles; to another prophecy; to another discerning of spirits; to another divers kinds of tongues; to another the interpretation of tongues:
11. But all these worketh that one and the selfsame Spirit, dividing to every man severally as he will.

Gal. 5:22-26
22. But the fruit of the Spirit is love, joy, peace, longsuffering, gentleness, goodness, faith,
23. Meekness, temperance: against such there is no law.
24. And they that are Christ's have crucified the flesh with the affections and lusts.
25. If we live in the Spirit, let us also walk in the Spirit.
26. Let us not be desirous of vain glory, provoking one another, envying one another.

Everybody has the gifts. Everybody can operate in them. The whole body of Christ, on the earth.

It is the same with the fruit of the spirit.

Let's say a man is 30 or 40 years old when he received Jesus in his heart. He is pretty much set in his ways. Unyielding in some areas and insistent in others. Self-centered, thinking it's all about him and his needs.

Psa. 1:3
And he shall be like a tree planted by the rivers of water, that bringeth forth his fruit in his season; his leaf also shall not wither; and whatsoever he doeth shall prosper.

After he receives Jesus as saviour, it may take years, or just a few days for him to bear his fruit, but in his season….he will.

(v.22) But the fruit of the Spirit is love, joy, peace, longsuffering, gentleness, goodness, faith,

(v.23) Meekness, temperance: against such there is no law.

These fruits are for the people around you. your co-workers, family, church members, and strangers you don't even know. You show forth the love of God.

Yesterday I worked diligently to find the link that wouldn't let Week-3-Day-3 post. I found it, it was a scripture. It was Eph. 3:10, but you're going to have to read it for yourself.

Mt. 12:33-35
33. Either make the tree good, and his fruit good; or else make the tree corrupt, and his fruit corrupt: for the tree is known by his fruit.
34. O generation of vipers, how can ye, being evil, speak good things? for out of the abundance of the heart the mouth speaketh.
35. A good man out of the good treasure of the heart bringeth forth good things: and an evil man out of the evil treasure bringeth forth evil things.

Jo. 15:16
Ye have not chosen me, but I have chosen you, and ordained you, that ye should go and bring forth fruit, and that your fruit should remain: that whatsoever ye shall ask of the Father in my

name, he may give it you.

The Bible is like a mirror. An odd mirror, that doesn't show what we look like, but the way God sees us. As we gaze into that mirror, we slowly turn into the image we see. As we see Christ, we turn into being Christ-like, unto the stature of the fullness of Christ!! No more tossed to and fro by every wind of doctrine, but knowing what the will of God is.

Jo. 14:12
Verily, verily, I say unto you, He that believeth on me, the works that I do shall he do also; and greater works than these shall he do; because I go unto my Father.

We are supposed to be a bunch of little exact duplicates of Jesus walking around on the earth healing the sick, raising the dead, and meeting the needs of the people.

Lk. 4:18-19
18. The Spirit of the Lord is upon me, because he hath anointed me to preach the gospel to the poor; he hath sent me to heal the brokenhearted, to preach deliverance to the captives, and recovering of sight to the blind, to set at liberty them that are bruised,
19. To preach the acceptable year of the Lord.

Are you in Jesus? Then put on Jesus!! We need to cop an attitude. It is no longer I that liveth, but Christ that liveth in me....He doeth the works!!

I have learned of Him. His yoke is easy and His burden is light.

My prayer is this, Lord, I don't understand, I don't see how this can possibly be, nevertheless at thy Word, I will speak to the mountain, I will speak to the tree. I will call those things that be not… as though they were. I will rest under the shadow of your wings, in the quietness of your Spirit, and know that you are God. I will walk in the fullness of my calling, and the power of my gifts, and in the authority of YOUR KINGDOM. O Lord, let the truth of YOUR KINGDOM reign in me, Amen.

If you can pray that prayer with me, you are well on your way into the "Knowledge" of The KINGDOM. We are living in the most exciting time in the history of mankind. I believe the Lord is looking for a few good men in these final days. Trained, equipped, and prepared for service.

As for myself, I don't want to be a bystander, I want to be used in these last days.

Lk. 12:32
Fear not, little flock; for it is your Father's good pleasure to give you the kingdom.

Rejoice, for the time of our redemption is near.

●●●

Day - 3
"The Perfecting of the Saints"
(Ephesians 4:12-16)

Kingdom Seekers
WEEK 7 DAY 3
01-29-2014

Eph. 4:11-16
11. And he gave some, apostles; and some, prophets; and some, evangelists; and some, pastors and teachers;
12. For the perfecting of the saints, for the work of the ministry, for the edifying of the body of Christ:
13. Till we all come in the unity of the faith, and of the knowledge of the Son of God, unto a perfect man, unto the measure of the stature of the fulness of Christ:
14. That we henceforth be no more children, tossed to and fro, and carried about with every wind of doctrine, by the sleight of men, and cunning craftiness, whereby they lie in wait to deceive;
15. But speaking the truth in love, may grow up into him in all things, which is the head, even Christ:
16. From whom the whole body fitly joined together and compacted by that which every joint supplieth, according to the effectual working in the measure of every part, maketh increase of the body unto the edifying of itself in love.

There are so many messages out there that have nothing to do with the life that God has prepared for those who love Him.

What does human behavior have to do with eternal life? God has dealt with that!! Completely!!

God didn't just set the law aside, He fulfilled it. While we were yet sinners, we have been perfected forever, through Christ's death, burial, and resurrection.

For now, as for the Kingdom realities in this world, we need to learn some things. Touch not, taste not, handle not, has nothing to do with the Kingdom on the earth. Having begun in the spirit, we are NOT made perfect by the flesh.

Jesus said,
Jo. 6:63
It is the spirit that quickeneth; the flesh profiteth nothing: the words that I speak unto you, they are spirit, and they are life.

You know what?

When Paul said in
Php. 3:10a
That I may know him, and the power of his resurrection...

I can't help but wonder which resurrection he was talking about. The similitude, or the actual?

Jesus did no ministry or miracle before He was baptized, yet after baptism He began his ministry. Something tells me that there is more about water baptism than we've been taught.

Now let's consider the actual Death, Burial, and Resurrection. Jesus is healing the sick, raising the dead and meeting the needs of the people with signs, wonders, and miracles. But Wait....He was doing that after the similitude, as well as after the actual Death, Burial, and Resurrection.

Hey...He hasn't changed. He is the same yesterday, today, and tomorrow.

Ro. 6:4-5
4. Therefore we are buried with him by baptism into death: that like as Christ was raised up from the dead by the glory of the Father, even so we also should walk in newness of life.
5. For if we have been planted together in the likeness of his death, we shall be also in the likeness of his resurrection:

Could it be that water baptism is a type of "right of passage" into the power of His resurrection?

"For the Perfecting of the Saints," FOR THE WORK OF THE MINISTRY….. Oh…Oh… Hhhmmmmm…Yes…. For the work of the ministry…yes….could be??

Water baptism, now there's a subject to be investigated. The Bible teaches that water baptism is for the forgiveness of sins.

Mk. 1:4
John did baptize in the wilderness, and preach the baptism of repentance for the remission of sins.

(Also read Lk. 3:3 and Col. 2:6-16)

I could explain it but this passage explains itself perfectly. Don't be moved by natural behavior, it is the sin nature of the flesh doing that…not you.

Hammering you on natural behavior will not build you up to any, state of maturity. The Word….will.

Act. 1:22
Beginning from the baptism of John, unto that same day that he was taken up from us, must one be ordained to be a witness with us of his resurrection.

Okay, let's go through this step by step.

Beginning from the baptism of John, we are focusing on the beginning of Jesus' ministry, unto that same day that he was taken up from us. This includes the entire ministry of Jesus on the earth, showing forth the "power" of His resurrection, after the "similitude" of His death, burial, and resurrection.

Do you realize that we go through the same similitude when we are baptized? Could it be at that point, (water baptism) that we "qualify" for the Jesus type of ministry in our own earthly ministry?

If we knew it, we would do it. But unfortunately, we don't know it because the Bible teaches baptism is for the remission of sins, not that we now qualify for any kind of ministry, or gifts.

Let me ask you this, did Jesus have any sin to be remitted?

No!! He submitted to water baptism, in order to fulfill all righteousness.

1 Co. 10:1-4
1. Moreover, brethren, I would not that ye should be ignorant, how that all our fathers were under the cloud, and all passed through the sea;
2. And were all baptized unto Moses in the cloud and in the sea;
3. And did all eat the same spiritual meat;
4. And did all drink the same spiritual drink: for they drank of that spiritual Rock that followed them: and that Rock was Christ.

I'm running out of room, read on through verse 12 in your Bible.

For the remission of sins might just be an OT feature, whereas the Fulfillment of all Righteousness is a NT Truth.

We will investigate this water baptism issue in Week 11.

Jesus did say to the woman caught in adultery, go and sin no more. I believe righteousness was imputed to her because she believed Jesus was the Christ. She and all the disciples and all who believed on Jesus at the time…righteousness was imputed to them.

Isn't it great! Sin is behind us, not shackled to us like a ball and chain. We are dead to sin and alive to God through Christ Jesus. Where no law is, there is no transgression.

Walk in what you know!!

God has condemned sin in the flesh so that it can no longer Lord it over us and condemn us. That's good news!!

Let me encourage you to keep up with Kingdom Seekers, I won't hammer you on what you do, I will only encourage you, for who you are in Christ.

Walk as children of light. Walk in what you know.

The rest will come.

Lk. 12:32
Fear not, little flock; for it is your Father's good pleasure to give you the kingdom.

●●●●

Day - 4
"The Stature of the Fullness of Christ"
(Ephesians 4:13)

Kingdom Seekers
WEEK 7 DAY 4
01-30-2014

Eph. 4:13
Till we all come in the unity of the faith, and of the knowledge of the Son of God, unto a perfect man, unto the measure of the stature of the fulness of Christ:

Okay, let's get wordy here. We need to understand this verse.

▶ #1. "Till we all come in the unity of the faith,"---- That is to say, believing on the Lord Jesus unto salvation, then, to believe on His name as a way of life.

Ro. 1:17
For therein is the righteousness of God revealed from faith to faith: as it is written, The just shall live by faith.

...and
1 Jo. 5:13
These things have I written unto you that believe on the name of the Son of God; that ye may know that ye have eternal life, and that ye may believe on the name of the Son of God.

Now that you have believed on the name unto salvation, you may now believe on the name as a way of life; to get your needs met, to get your prayers answered, to a living wage job, to get your home, to send your kids through school, to deal with the issues of life!!!

►#2. "and of the knowledge of the Son of God,"----

Jo. 17:17
Sanctify them through thy truth: thy word is truth.

Jo. 8:31-32
31. Then said Jesus to those Jews which believed on him, If ye continue in my word, then are ye my disciples indeed;
32. And ye shall know the truth, and the truth shall make you free.

Jo. 16:13-15
13. Howbeit when he, the Spirit of truth, is come, he will guide you into all truth: for he shall not speak of himself; but whatsoever he shall hear, that shall he speak: and he will show you things to come.
14. He shall glorify me: for he shall receive of mine, and shall show it unto you.
15. All things that the Father hath are mine: therefore said I, that he shall take of mine, and shall show it unto you.

The knowledge of the Son of God.

Jesus said, My words, they are spirit, and they are life. Guard your heart with all diligence, for out of it, are the issues of life.

Lk. 6:45
A good man out of the good treasure of his heart bringeth forth that which is good; and an evil man out of the evil treasure of his heart bringeth forth that which is evil: for of the abundance of the heart his mouth speaketh.

►#3. "unto a perfect man,"---- #5046 in Strong's concordance. Teleios *(tel-I-os)* growth, completeness, of full age, perfect.

Heb. 5:12-14
12. For when for the time ye ought to be teachers, ye have need that one teach you again which be the first principles of the oracles of God; and are become such as have need of milk, and not of strong meat.
13. For every one that useth milk is unskilful in the word of righteousness: for he is a babe.
14. But strong meat belongeth to them that are of full age, even those who by reason of use have their senses exercised to discern both good and evil.

Did you notice, unskilful in the word of righteousness?

That's what God calls the faith walk of today. The Word of righteousness.

►#4. "unto the measure"---- #3358. Metron *(met-ron)* measure, limited portion, or degree.

Ro. 12:3-8

3. For I say, through the grace given unto me, to every man that is among you, not to think of himself more highly than he ought to think; but to think soberly, according as God hath dealt to every man the measure of faith.

4. For as we have many members in one body, and all members have not the same office:

5. So we, being many, are one body in Christ, and every one members one of another.

6. Having then gifts differing according to the grace that is given to us, whether prophecy, let us prophesy according to the proportion of faith;

7. Or ministry, let us wait on our ministering: or he that teacheth, on teaching;

8. Or he that exhorteth, on exhortation: he that giveth, let him do it with simplicity; he that ruleth, with diligence; he that showeth mercy, with cheerfulness.

Mk. 4:21-25

21. And he said unto them, Is a candle brought to be put under a bushel, or under a bed? and not to be set on a candlestick?

22. For there is nothing hid, which shall not be manifested; neither was any thing kept secret, but that it should come abroad.

23. If any man have ears to hear, let him hear.

24. And he said unto them, Take heed what ye hear: with what measure ye mete, it shall be measured to you: and unto you that hear shall more be given.

25. For he that hath, to him shall be given: and he that hath not, from him shall be taken even that which he hath.

▶ **#5.** "of the stature"---- #2244. helikia *(hay-lik-ee-ah)* maturity, years, size, age, stature.

Heb. 5:12-14. For when for the time ye ought to be teachers…

▶ **#6.** "of the fulness"---- # 4138 pleroma *(play-ro-mah)* what is filled, which is put in to fill up, full, fullness.

When your bucket is bumped, what comes out?

What the world has taught you, or what your Heavenly Father has taught you?

If you don't know that much about God…READ THE BOOK!!

He loves you. He's made a way for you to succeed in life.

Mt. 11:28-30

28. Come unto me, all ye that labour and are heavy laden, and I will give you rest.

29. Take my yoke upon you, and learn of me; for I am meek and lowly in heart: and ye shall find rest unto your souls.

30. For my yoke is easy, and my burden is light.

Lk. 12:32
Fear not, little flock; for it is your Father's good pleasure to give you the kingdom.

Tomorrow, "Tithes and offerings" Yeaaaaahhh….

What?

• • • • •

Day - 5
"Tithes and Offerings"
(Malachi 3:7-12)

Kingdom Seekers
WEEK 7 DAY 5
01-31-2014

Mal. 3:7-12
7. Even from the days of your fathers ye are gone away from mine ordinances, and have not kept them. Return unto me, and I will return unto you, saith the LORD of hosts. But ye said, Wherein shall we return?
8. Will a man rob God? Yet ye have robbed me. But ye say, Wherein have we robbed thee? In tithes and offerings.
9. Ye are cursed with a curse: for ye have robbed me, even this whole nation.
10. Bring ye all the tithes into the storehouse, that there may be meat in mine house, and prove me now herewith, saith the LORD of hosts, if I will not open you the windows of heaven, and pour you out a blessing, that there shall not be room enough to receive it.
11. And I will rebuke the devourer for your sakes, and he shall not destroy the fruits of your ground; neither shall your vine cast her fruit before the time in the field, saith the LORD of hosts.
12. And all nations shall call you blessed: for ye shall be a delightsome land, saith the LORD of hosts.

First of all, let me point out that I don't receive tithes or offerings.

What I'm about to share with you is the truth of what God has shown me about tithes and offerings.

The tithes go into the local church. Period!! Not to some televangelist, pet project, or a man on Facebook like me.

Offerings are another thing. People inevitably equate offerings with money, but that's not always true. Offerings can be in the form of time, food, clothing, paying the electric bill for someone this month, or something as simple as mowing the grass for somebody.

God considers withholding the tithe as robbery. Why?

Because it was law?

No. The tithe was instituted 400 years before the law was given. The tithe was incorporated into the law, but it was a law unto itself for the support of the church and the priesthood. The tribe of Levi did not receive an inheritance in the promised land….they received the tithe! They took care of church business and lived off the tithe.

The tithe is God's economic system. Let me share an illustrated sermon a preacher told once.

He asked the congregation how many had received their dividend check this month from General Motors.

No one raised their hand.

He said, "What, nobody got their check this month? Do you know why, you didn't get a check this month? I'll tell you why, you don't have any stock in General Motors, that's why you didn't get a check. You don't qualify to get a check. You're not involved with G.M."

If you're not a tither, you're not involved in God's economic system.

Look back at verse 9. You are cursed with a curse.

This is not to be confused with the curse of the law which we have been redeemed from. This is a curse on God's financial system on the earth.

Let's see if any of this sounds familiar,
Hag. 1:5-6
5. Now therefore thus saith the LORD of hosts; Consider your ways.
6. Ye have sown much, and bring in little; ye eat, but ye have not enough; ye drink, but ye are not filled with drink; ye clothe you, but there is none warm; and he that earneth wages earneth wages to put it into a bag with holes.

How much money do you have left over at the end of the month? Is your paycheck spent before you get it? Is any paycheck ever enough?

He goes on,
Hag. 1:7-11
7. Thus saith the LORD of hosts; Consider your ways.
8. Go up to the mountain, and bring wood, and build the house; and I will take pleasure in it, and I will be glorified, saith the LORD.
9. Ye looked for much, and, lo, it came to little; and when ye brought it home, I did blow upon it. Why? saith the LORD of hosts. Because of mine house that is waste, and ye run every man unto his own house.

10. Therefore the heaven over you is stayed from dew, and the earth is stayed from her fruit.

11. And I called for a drought upon the land, and upon the mountains, and upon the corn, and upon the new wine, and upon the oil, and upon that which the ground bringeth forth, and upon men, and upon cattle, and upon all the labour of the hands.

This is not a curse of the Law, it is a curse on finances. Separate from the Law.

If these curses sound familiar in your life, let me encourage you to get involved in God's economic system.

Look at *(v.10)*
Bring ye all the tithes into the storehouse, that there may be meat in mine house, and prove me now herewith, saith the LORD of hosts, if I will not open you the windows of heaven, and pour you out a blessing, that there shall not be room enough to receive it.

Open the windows of heaven…pour you out a blessing…not room enough to receive ..sounds good to me!!

(v.11)
And I will rebuke the devourer for your sakes, and he shall not destroy the fruits of your ground; neither shall your vine cast her fruit before the time in the field, saith the LORD of hosts.

Do these three promises sound awkward to you?

They did to me until I realized that, in The KINGDOM of GOD, we live in an agrarian society, we sow, and we reap. We sow words, and we reap the fruit of the words that we sowed.

You may not understand this last statement. Let me encourage you to look back at the earlier messages. Weeks 2, 3, 4, and 5.

Gal. 6:7-9
7. Be not deceived; God is not mocked: for whatsoever a man soweth, that shall he also reap.
8. For he that soweth to his flesh shall of the flesh reap corruption; but he that soweth to the Spirit shall of the Spirit reap life everlasting.
9. And let us not be weary in well doing: for in due season we shall reap, if we faint not.]

Don't forget,
So is the kingdom of God, as if a man should cast seed into the ground; And should sleep, and rise night and day, and the seed should spring and grow up, he knoweth not how. For the earth bringeth forth fruit of herself; first the blade, then the ear, after that the full corn in the ear.

2 Co. 9:10
Now he that ministereth seed to the sower both minister bread for your food, and multiply your

seed sown, and increase the fruits of your righteousness;)

Isa. 55:10b
...that it may give seed to the sower, and bread to the eater:

Lk. 12:32
Fear not, little flock; for it is your Father's good pleasure to give you the kingdom.

• NOTES •
God's Economics

There is a New Testament equivalent to the windows of heaven blessing of

Mal. 3:10
Bring ye all the tithes into the storehouse, that there may be meat in mine house, and prove me now herewith, saith the LORD of hosts, if I will not open you the windows of heaven, and pour you out a blessing, that there shall not be room enough to receive it.

You will find it in
Lu. 6:38
Give, and it shall be given unto you; good measure, pressed down, and shaken together, and running over, shall men give into your bosom. For with the same measure that ye mete withal it shall be measured to you again.

Good measure…pressed down.. Shaken together…and running over. You can't beat that with interest, compounded daily!! This promise is given in the category of offerings, not Tithes.

For with the same measure that ye mete withal it shall be measured to you again.

God's economic system starts with the Tithe, and is filled with abundant returns. These are not the only ways that God can provide financial help.

Lk. 6:35
But love ye your enemies, and do good, and lend, hoping for nothing again; and your reward shall be great, and ye shall be the children of the Highest: for he is kind unto the unthankful and to the evil.

Hoping for nothing again… the inference here is that God, will take care of you.

Lu. 14:12-14
12. Then said he also to him that bade him, When thou makest a dinner or a supper, call not thy friends, nor thy brethren, neither thy kinsmen, nor thy rich neighbours; lest they also bid thee again, and a recompense be made thee.

13. But when thou makest a feast, call the poor, the maimed, the lame, the blind:

14. And thou shalt be blessed; for they cannot recompense thee: for thou shalt be recompensed at the resurrection of the just.

Don't go to thinking that those you gave to, will repay. At the end of the day, after you have given to those who cannot repay, God will recompense.

2 Co. 9:6-11

6. But this I say, He which soweth sparingly shall reap also sparingly; and he which soweth bountifully shall reap also bountifully. (God is a multiplier of seed sown. If you give a spoon full, God's spoon is bigger than your spoon. If you give a shovel full, God's shovel is bigger than your shovel.)

7. Every man according as he purposeth in his heart, so let him give; not grudgingly, or of necessity: for God loveth a cheerful giver. (Don't think you must give till it hurts. There are those who will say, give us your "best gift" this month. They're only feeding their machine. They're only tending a pet project that they have created that takes hundreds, or thousands a month to operate. They're not looking to God to provide, but put the pressure on you, don't fall for it. If God is behind their project, He will provide.)

8. And God is able to make all grace abound toward you; that ye, always having all sufficiency in all things, may abound to every good work: (It is God's will that you have enough for yourself and plenty to give out to meet the need of others, having all sufficiency in all things, in need of no assistance from anybody for anything, that you may abound to every good work.)

9. (As it is written, He hath dispersed abroad; he hath given to the poor: his righteousness remaineth for ever

10. Now he that ministereth seed to the sower both minister bread for your food, and multiply your seed sown, and increase the fruits of your righteousness;)

11. Being enriched in every thing to all bountifulness, which causeth through us thanksgiving to God.

Come on church, I'll say it again, let's get on the other side of this learning curve. God has prepared a wonderful life for us, get involved, be blessed.

Prv. 19:17

He that hath pity upon the poor lendeth unto the LORD; and that which he hath given will he pay him again.

Here we see that if you give a dollar, God will give you back a dollar.

Mk. 4:23-24

23. If any man have ears to hear, let him hear.

24. And he said unto them, Take heed what ye hear: with what measure ye mete, it shall be measured to you: and unto you that hear shall more be given.

God has given us a way to live a bountiful life. Get in line with the Word. Jesus said it this way, I am come that they might have life, and that they might have it more abundantly. I am the Way, the Truth, and the Life. Words!! Words, that are able to produce themselves in the form of whatever they state, indicate, or describe.

Isa. 55:10-11
10. For as the rain cometh down, and the snow from heaven, and returneth not thither, but watereth the earth, and maketh it bring forth and bud, that it may give seed to the sower, and bread to the eater:
11. So shall my word be that goeth forth out of my mouth: it shall not return unto me void, but it shall accomplish that which I please, and it shall prosper in the thing whereto I sent it.

Can you see it? The Word of God is designed to produce a result, or harvest of what it says or describes.

Heb. 4:12
For the word of God is quick, and powerful, and sharper than any twoedged sword, piercing even to the dividing asunder of soul and spirit, and of the joints and marrow, and is a discerner of the thoughts and intents of the heart.

The Word of God now dwells in you. Ask what you will, and it shall be done unto you. I didn't say that, Jesus did in
Jo. 15:7
If ye abide in me, and my words abide in you, ye shall ask what ye will, and it shall be done unto you.

Jo. 16:24
Hitherto have ye asked nothing in my name: ask, and ye shall receive, that your joy may be full.

There's more, a lot more but this is enough for now. Enough for us to begin the journey into God's abundant life.

Lk. 12:32
Fear not, little flock; for it is your Father's good pleasure to give you the kingdom.

■ □ ■ □ ■ □ ■ □

Week-8
Exhortation to Maturity

Week-8-Days-1-5
Exhortation to Maturity:
Day-1. The Five Warnings of Hebrews. Heb. 2, 3, 5, 10 & 12
Day-2. Once Enlightened. Heb. 6:4-9
Day-3. The Sincere Milk of the Word. 1 Pet. 2:2
Day-4. Study to Show Yourself Approved. 2 Tim. 2:15
Day-5. When I Was a Child. 1 Co. 13:11

•

Day - 1
"The Five Warnings of Hebrews"
(Hebrews 2-3, 5, 10, 12)

Kingdom Seekers
WEEK 8 DAY 1
02-03-2014

This is an exhortation to maturity. These warnings are to be taken seriously, and should cause us to proceed carefully.

■ **1st Warning. "Neglect:"**

Heb. 2:1-4
1. Therefore we ought to give the more earnest heed to the things which we have heard, lest at any time we should let them slip.
2. For if the word spoken by angels was stedfast, and every transgression and disobedience received a just recompense of reward;
3. How shall we escape, if we neglect so great salvation; which at the first began to be spoken by the Lord, and was confirmed unto us by them that heard him;
4. God also bearing them witness, both with signs and wonders, and with divers miracles, and gifts of the Holy Ghost, according to his own will?

Jesus was going about healing the sick and doing good for the people. He was also teaching and preaching the gospel of The KINGDOM. God was backing Him up with signs, wonders, and miracles, and gifts of the Holy Ghost.

■ **2nd Warning. "Unbelief:"**   *(Read; Heb. 3:1-19 and 4:1-16)*

Heb. 3:19
So we see that they could not enter in because of unbelief.

You may not know this but the gospel was preached to Abraham way back when, and the gospel was preached to the children of Israel in the wilderness, but not being mixed with faith, it didn't profit them anything.

Eze. 34:4
The diseased have ye not strengthened, neither have ye healed that which was sick, neither have ye bound up that which was broken, neither have ye brought again that which was driven away, neither have ye sought that which was lost; but with force and with cruelty have ye ruled them.

Because of unbelief they could not do these things, so they did not do these things.

Eze. 34:10
Thus saith the Lord GOD; Behold, I am against the shepherds; and I will require my flock at their hand, and cause them to cease from feeding the flock; neither shall the shepherds feed them-selves any more; for I will deliver my flock from their mouth, that they may not be meat for them.

Jesus said in
Mt. 21:43
Therefore say I unto you, The kingdom of God shall be taken from you, and given to a nation bringing forth the fruits thereof.

■ **3rd Warning. "Not Maturing:"**

Heb. 5:12-14
12. For when for the time ye ought to be teachers, ye have need that one teach you again which be the first principles of the oracles of God; and are become such as have need of milk, and not of strong meat.
13. For every one that useth milk is unskilful in the word of righteousness: for he is a babe.
14. But strong meat belongeth to them that are of full age, even those who by reason of use have their senses exercised to discern both good and evil.

■ **4th Warning. "Drawing Back:"**

Heb. 10:26-39
26. For if we sin wilfully after that we have received the knowledge of the truth, there remaineth no more sacrifice for sins,

27. But a certain fearful looking for of judgment and fiery indignation, which shall devour the adversaries.

28. He that despised Moses' law died without mercy under two or three witnesses:

29. Of how much sorer punishment, suppose ye, shall he be thought worthy, who hath trodden under foot the Son of God, and hath counted the blood of the covenant, wherewith he was sanctified, an unholy thing, and hath done despite unto the Spirit of grace?

30. For we know him that hath said, Vengeance belongeth unto me, I will recompense, saith the Lord. And again, The Lord shall judge his people.

31. It is a fearful thing to fall into the hands of the living God.

32. But call to remembrance the former days, in which, after ye were illuminated, ye endured a great fight of afflictions;

33. Partly, whilst ye were made a gazingstock both by reproaches and afflictions; and partly, whilst ye became companions of them that were so used.

34. For ye had compassion of me in my bonds, and took joyfully the spoiling of your goods, knowing in yourselves that ye have in heaven a better and an enduring substance.

35. Cast not away therefore your confidence, which hath great recompense of reward.

36. For ye have need of patience, that, after ye have done the will of God, ye might receive the promise.

37. For yet a little while, and he that shall come will come, and will not tarry.

38. Now the just shall live by faith: but if any man draw back, my soul shall have no pleasure in him.

39. But we are not of them who draw back unto perdition; but of them that believe to the saving of the soul.

After we have been illuminated, if we draw back unto perdition, and sin willfully, there is no new sacrifice.

The just shall live by Faith.

Ro. 8:29-31

29. For whom he did foreknow, he also did predestinate to be conformed to the image of his Son, that he might be the firstborn among many brethren.

30. Moreover whom he did predestinate, them he also called: and whom he called, them he also justified: and whom he justified, them he also glorified.

31. What shall we then say to these things? If God be for us, who can be against us?

We are to be changed from glory to glory into the image that we see in the Word, unto the stature of the fullness of Christ. How do we do it? By being renewed in knowledge after the image of Him that created him. (in Righteousness and true Holiness)

■ **5th Warning. "Refusing God:"**

Heb. 12:25-29

25. See that ye refuse not him that speaketh. For if they escaped not who refused him that spake on earth, much more shall not we escape, if we turn away from him that speaketh from heaven:

26. *Whose voice then shook the earth: but now he hath promised, saying, Yet once more I shake not the earth only, but also heaven.*

27. *And this word, Yet once more, signifieth the removing of those things that are shaken, as of things that are made, that those things which cannot be shaken may remain.*

28. *Wherefore we receiving a kingdom which cannot be moved, let us have grace, whereby we may serve God acceptably with reverence and godly fear:*

29. *For our God is a consuming fire. For it is impossible for us who were once enlightened, and have tasted of the heavenly gift, and were made partakers of the Holy Ghost,*

Heb. 6:5
And have tasted the good word of God, and the powers of the world to come, If we shall fall away, to renew ourselves again unto repentance; seeing we crucify to ourselves the Son of God afresh, and put him to an open shame.

Lk. 12:32
Fear not, little flock; for it is your Father's good pleasure to give you the kingdom.

●●

Day - 2
"Once Enlightened"
(Hebrews 6:4-9)

Kingdom Seekers
WEEK 8 DAY 2
02-04-2014

Heb. 6:4-9
4. *For it is impossible for those who were once enlightened, and have tasted of the heavenly gift, and were made partakers of the Holy Ghost,*

5. *And have tasted the good word of God, and the powers of the world to come,*

6. *If they shall fall away, to renew them again unto repentance; seeing they crucify to themselves the Son of God afresh, and put him to an open shame.*

7. *For the earth which drinketh in the rain that cometh oft upon it, and bringeth forth herbs meet for them by whom it is dressed, receiveth blessing from God:*

8. *But that which beareth thorns and briers is rejected, and is nigh unto cursing; whose end is to be burned.*

9. *But, beloved, we are persuaded better things of you, and things that accompany salvation, though we thus speak.*

Not every denomination will bring a person to the point of being once enlightened. I know this because I was born again in one of them. I'm not knocking them though. They're on the front lines, and in the heat of the battle of reconciliation.

If you like a good read, read "The Final Quest" by Rick Joyner, and pray for these denominations that deny the power. They are sick and broke and they don't know what the will of God is for them.

One can read this passage of scripture two ways. It is impossible for people who were once enlightened to go back into the old way of life, living for the flesh, and not for the spirit. The other is, it is impossible to renew ourselves to repentance once we have been enlightened, because we crucify the Son of God afresh. There is no new sacrifice!!

Verse 7 is to be read from a "Kingdom" perspective.
(v.7) For the earth which drinketh in the rain that cometh oft upon it, and bringeth forth herbs meet for them by whom it is dressed, receiveth blessing from God.

Verse 7 shows us how we can take the Word of God, and sow it into our life situations and overcome them by the Word of our testimony, because when we do that, we receive blessing from God in the form of "answered prayer."

Reminiscent of
Isa. 55:10-11
10. For as the rain cometh down, and the snow from heaven, and returneth not thither, but watereth the earth, and maketh it bring forth and bud, that it may give seed to the sower, and bread to the eater:
11. So shall my word be that goeth forth out of my mouth: it shall not return unto me void, but it shall accomplish that which I please, and it shall prosper in the thing whereto I sent it.

The Word of God is designed to produce itself. What is it designed to produce? What it says, describes, or what was intended, when it was spoken.

What promise are you standing on, for your breakthrough? That's what will be made manifest.

First the blade, then the ear, after that, the full corn in the ear. That's how The KINGDOM of GOD works.

Mk. 4:26-28
26. So is the kingdom of God, as if a man should cast seed into the ground;
27. And should sleep, and rise night and day, and the seed should spring and grow up, he knoweth not how.
28. For the earth bringeth forth fruit of herself;

If you just joined Kingdom Seekers, you need to go back to Weeks 2, 3, 4, 5, and 6 in order to fully understand what we're seeing today.

Once we know how the system works, we can work the system.

Our words have power! What power? The power to produce themselves in this natural realm. Calling those things that be not, as though they were.

Like a baby horse colt born 5 minutes ago, a person newly born again already has everything he or she will ever need already inside them. The Kingdom of God is within us.

Our wealth is not in the form of money, or silver, or gold. Our wealth is more precious than that. Our wealth is outrageous in it's buying power, and dynamic in it's working. Outrageous, because we buy and acquire without money, and without price.

Our wealth is in the form of "words." Not just any words, but Faith filled Words, accompanied with Faith, forethought, intent, and expectation. Note: If you're expecting what you said will actually happen, that's Faith!! If you're not expecting, you're not in Faith.

Well how do our words come to pass?

Jesus said in
Jo. 14:13-14
13. And whatsoever ye shall ask in my name, that will I do, that the Father may be glorified in the Son.
14. If ye shall ask any thing in my name, I WILL DO IT.

Jesus does everything God says. Jesus is the creative power of God. Jesus is The Word of God.

Jo. 1:3
1. In the beginning was the Word, and the Word was with God, and the Word was God.
2. The same was in the beginning with God.
3. All things were made by him; and without him was not any thing made that was made.

Okay, so how do things manifest in this natural realm?

Mk. 16:20
And they went forth, and preached every where, "the Lord working with them, and confirming the word with signs following." Amen.

Are you illuminated yet? Do you see that it was the Word, on salvation that saved you? How was that done? Simple, the Word was made flesh, took upon Himself our sin, died on the cross, paid the price for our sin, and rose again for our justification. We are born again "in Him."

It's the Word that will produce what we need. Study the promises. What do you need? What do you want in life? Speak it, doubt not in your heart, but believe for it, and you shall have it!!

Ro. 8:29-32

29. For whom he did foreknow, he also did predestinate to be conformed to the image of his Son, that he might be the firstborn among many brethren.

30. Moreover whom he did predestinate, them he also called: and whom he called, them he also justified: and whom he justified, them he also glorified.

31. What shall we then say to these things? If God be for us, who can be against us?

32. He that spared not his own Son, but delivered him up for us all, how shall he not with him also freely give us all things?

●●●

Day - 3
"The Sincere Milk of the Word"
(I Peter 2:2)

Kingdom Seekers
WEEK 8 DAY 3
02-05-2014

1 Pet. 2:1-3

1. Wherefore laying aside all malice, and all guile, and hypocrisies, and envies, and all evil speakings,

2. As newborn babes, desire the sincere milk of the word, that ye may grow thereby:

3. If so be ye have tasted that the Lord is gracious.

You know what, I've been a Christian all my life but I remained a babe in Christ until I was in my late forties. I didn't know anything about God, His Son, His Spirit, or His KINGDOM. But the day came that I was fed up with not being fed up. So I started reading my Bible for myself, instead of taking a preacher's word on what the Bible says. Guess what, I began to see a different interpretation. The Bible was speaking to me as an individual. Its message was not the same as what my pastor was telling me. I was born again in a denomination that knows salvation frontwards, backwards, side to side, and top to bottom, but they don't seem to know anything else for sure.

Heb. 6:12-14

12. For when for the time ye ought to be teachers, ye have need that one teach you again which be the first principles of the oracles of God; and are become such as have need of milk, and not of strong meat.

13. For every one that useth milk is unskilful in the word of righteousness: for he is a babe.

14. But strong meat belongeth to them that are of full age, even those who by reason of use have their senses exercised to discern both good and evil.

Heb. 6:1-3

1. Therefore leaving the principles of the doctrine of Christ, let us go on unto perfection; not lay-

ing again the foundation of repentance from dead works, and of faith toward God,

2. Of the doctrine of baptisms, and of laying on of hands, and of resurrection of the dead, and of eternal judgment.

3. And this will we do, if God permit.

What we're seeing here is what the writer calls the milk of the Word. We are all a product of what we've been taught. If your Bible says one thing and your pastor is saying something else, I'd get out of that church!!

The denomination I was attending would skip over the active, or power verses. Mt. 21:22, Mk. 11:24, Jo. 15:7, and such were never mentioned in my church. Mt. 21:21, Mk. 11:23, and Jo. 14:13-14 may have been read, but never expounded on.

I had to go to a "Christian Center" instead of a denominational church because denominational doctrine doesn't always include Bible Truth.

Acts 17:2-6
2. And Paul, as his manner was, went in unto them, and three sabbath days reasoned with them out of the scriptures,

3. Opening and alleging, that Christ must needs have suffered, and risen again from the dead; and that this Jesus, whom I preach unto you, is Christ.

4. And some of them believed, and consorted with Paul and Silas; and of the devout Greeks a great multitude, and of the chief women not a few.

5. But the Jews which believed not, moved with envy, took unto them certain lewd fellows of the baser sort, and gathered a company, and set all the city on an uproar, and assaulted the house of Jason, and sought to bring them out to the people.

6. And when they found them not, they drew Jason and certain brethren unto the rulers of the city, crying, These that have turned the world upside down are come hither also;

Yes, the truth of the Bible will turn the traditions and teachings of the world and religions upside down. Carnal and Spiritual just don't mix. There's no common ground.

1 Co. 2:1-16
1. And I, brethren, when I came to you, came not with excellency of speech or of wisdom, declaring unto you the testimony of God.

2. For I determined not to know any thing among you, save Jesus Christ, and him crucified.

3. And I was with you in weakness, and in fear, and in much trembling.

4. And my speech and my preaching was not with enticing words of man's wisdom, but in demonstration of the Spirit and of power:

5. That your faith should not stand in the wisdom of men, but in the power of God.

6. Howbeit we speak wisdom among them that are perfect: yet not the wisdom of this world, nor of the princes of this world, that come to nought:

7. But we speak the wisdom of God in a mystery, even the hidden wisdom, which God ordained before the world unto our glory:

8.Which none of the princes of this world knew: for had they known it, they would not have crucified the Lord of glory.

9. But as it is written, Eye hath not seen, nor ear heard, neither have entered into the heart of man, the things which God hath prepared for them that love him.

10. But God hath revealed them unto us by his Spirit: for the Spirit searcheth all things, yea, the deep things of God.

11. For what man knoweth the things of a man, save the spirit of man which is in him? even so the things of God knoweth no man, but the Spirit of God.

12. Now we have received, not the spirit of the world, but the spirit which is of God; that we might know the things that are freely given to us of God.

13. Which things also we speak, not in the words which man's wisdom teacheth, but which the Holy Ghost teacheth; comparing spiritual things with spiritual.

14. But the natural man receiveth not the things of the Spirit of God: for they are foolishness unto him: neither can he know them, because they are spiritually discerned.

15. But he that is spiritual judgeth all things, yet he himself is judged of no man.

16. For who hath known the mind of the Lord, that he may instruct him? But we have the mind of Christ.

Php. 2:12b-15
12b. ...work out your own salvation with fear and trembling.
13. For it is God which worketh in you both to will and to do of his good pleasure.
14. Do all things without murmurings and disputings:
15.That ye may be blameless and harmless, the sons of God, without rebuke, in the midst of a crooked and perverse nation, among whom ye shine as lights in the world;

Lk. 12:32
Fear not, little flock; for it is your Father's good pleasure to give you the kingdom.

●●●●

Day - 4
"Study to Show Yourself Approved"
(II Timothy 2:15)

Kingdom Seekers
WEEK 8 DAY 4
02-06-2014

2 Tim. 2:15
Study to show thyself approved unto God, a workman that needeth not to be ashamed, rightly dividing the word of truth.

Lean not to your own understanding.

Ro. 8:6-7
6. For to be carnally minded is death; but to be spiritually minded is life and peace.
7. Because the carnal mind is enmity against God: for it is not subject to the law of God, neither indeed can be.

Jesus said, it is the spirit that is quickened, the flesh profits nothing. 1 Co. 2:16. Tells us that we have the mind of Christ, so look at it this way, the carnal mind cannot look into the things of God because they are spiritually discerned. It takes the mind of Christ to understand the Bible.

NOT THE NEW KING JAMES VERSION, OR THE AMERICAN STANDARD, OR THE AMPLIFIED VERSIONS. They are all paraphrased versions of the original King James Version, AIMED AT THE CARNAL MIND OF REASON in an honest effort for us to understand the Bible. Not realizing that the carnal mind can't understand, neither can it know, the things of God for they are foolishness, to the carnal mind of reason.

Prv. 3:1-8
1. My son, forget not my law; but let thine heart keep my commandments:
2. For length of days, and long life, and peace, shall they add to thee.
3. Let not mercy and truth forsake thee: bind them about thy neck; write them upon the table of thine heart:
4. So shalt thou find favour and good understanding in the sight of God and man.
5. Trust in the LORD with all thine heart; and lean not unto thine own understanding.
6. In all thy ways acknowledge him, and he shall direct thy paths.
7. Be not wise in thine own eyes: fear the LORD, and depart from evil.
8. It shall be health to thy navel, and marrow to thy bones.

Nowhere in man's wisdom or teachings is it offered that we will be in health if we believe this way or that, but the Word of God does offer life, health, and prosperity.

You have a choice. Who are you going to follow? The world's ways, or God's ways? Don't just take your pastor's word for what the Bible says, get in there and read it for yourself. You might see that there is more to it than what your pastor said there was.

1 Co. 2:4-7
4. And my speech and my preaching was not with enticing words of man's wisdom, but in demonstration of the Spirit and of power:
5. That your faith should not stand in the wisdom of men, but in the power of God.
6. Howbeit we speak wisdom among them that are perfect: yet not the wisdom of this world, nor of the princes of this world, that come to nought:
7. But we speak the wisdom of God in a mystery, even the hidden wisdom, which God ordained before the world unto our glory:

Hidden wisdom. You're going to have to search it out for yourselves if your pastor is not teaching the truth of the Word of God. Dig deep!! Lay your foundation on a rock, The Rock!! The Word of God.

Remember!! In this Bible study we are talking about the Word, not so much about Jesus. Jesus, was made the head of the corner, a living stone, but the foundation is, was, and always will be "The Word of God." We are builded upon it /Him. Did you get it? We are founded on the foundation of the Word, which the man Jesus, is the corner stone. God's wisdom is our glory.

Prv. 4:20-23
20. My son, attend to my words; incline thine ear unto my sayings.
21. Let them not depart from thine eyes; keep them in the midst of thine heart.
22. For they are life unto those that find them, and health to all their flesh.
23. Keep thy heart with all diligence; for out of it are the issues of life.

See this passage this way,
(v.22)
For they are life unto those that find them, and health to all their flesh. That's life and health!!

(v.23)
Keep thy heart with all diligence; for out of it are the issues of life. That's prosperity!!

Lk. 6:43-49
43. For a good tree bringeth not forth corrupt fruit; neither doth a corrupt tree bring forth good fruit.
44. For every tree is known by his own fruit. For of thorns men do not gather figs, nor of a bramble bush gather they grapes.
45. A good man out of the good treasure of his heart bringeth forth that which is good; and an evil man out of the evil treasure of his heart bringeth forth that which is evil: for of the abundance of the heart his mouth speaketh.
46. And why call ye me, Lord, Lord, and do not the things which I say?
47. Whosoever cometh to me, and heareth my sayings, and doeth them, I will show you to whom he is like:
48. He is like a man which built an house, and digged deep, and laid the foundation on a rock: and when the flood arose, the stream beat vehemently upon that house, and could not shake it: for it was founded upon a rock.
49. But he that heareth, and doeth not, is like a man that without a foundation built an house upon the earth; against which the stream did beat vehemently, and immediately it fell; and the ruin of that house was great.

I always thought that Jesus was talking about a believer and an unbeliever. But, no! Jesus is talking about two believers. One did the Word, and the other didn't. One stood, the other fell.

We have a choice, we can hunker down and "take"….. whatever comes, or we can "dictate" whatever we want to come. It's our choice. If we knew we were in charge of our lives, things would be different for us today. The thing is…we "are" in charge, and don't know it.

We simply don't recognize our true wealth. It's in the form of Words…not Silver or Gold, money or tools and equipment. It's Words only, in The KINGDOM of GOD, and we have a never ending supply at our disposal. All we'll ever need!!

Does the Bible actually say that Words are the true riches, the only rate of exchange in the Kingdom? NO! But according to what the Bible does say, there is no other conclusion that we can make. *(Read; Mt. 21:21-22, Mk. 11:23-24, Jo. 14:13-14; 15:7; 16:23-24)*

Lk. 12:32
Fear not, little flock; for it is your Father's good pleasure to give you the kingdom.

●●●●●

Day - 5
"When I Was a Child"
(I Corinthians 13:11)

Kingdom Seekers
WEEK 8 DAY 5
02-07-2014

1 Co. 13:11-12
11. When I was a child, I spake as a child, I understood as a child, I thought as a child: but when I became a man, I put away childish things.
12. For now we see through a glass, darkly; but then face to face: now I know in part; but then shall I know even as also I am known.

One thing is for sure, we all start as new-born babes.

When we are babes in Christ, we don't even realize that we need to learn how talk, just like we had to learn how to talk in the natural. Yes, we need to learn how to talk Spiritually.

Jesus said in
Jo. 6:63
It is the spirit that quickeneth; the flesh profiteth nothing: the words that I speak unto you, they are spirit, and they are life.

We need to learn how to talk that way. Oh hey, we know how to talk the way the world talks. "When the lay-off starts, I'll be the first one out the door." The flu season is here, I'll be the first one in my family to get it. We never win anything. What's the use, it won't work. Just as sure as we get there, they'll be sold out. Need I go on?

When we need money, we go to a bank or some financial company. When we need medical attention, we go to a doctor and or a hospital. When we need car work done, we go to a mechanic. Teeth work, a dentist, paint work, a painter, and so on, and so on.

We know how to deal with all kinds of situations in this natural realm. We're full of speculations, surmising's, and I guess this is the way it goes, I don't know.

Man's knowledge is so flaky, it changes every time a university does a new study. Even the medical profession is full of shaky flaky practices. I'm not complaining, I'm just saying. Pharmaceuticals, hey we have pills that are made for specific things but with a long lists of side effects, some even life threatening. Outrageous, but that's what we have to deal with in the world.

There are no guarantees. There are no sure fire ways of doing things.

Though we might find that kind of talk in the Bible, that's certainly not the way God talks. Everything He says gives hope, encouragement, confidence, and He blesses us with an abundance of promises that He want's to make good on for us. You know, when we get down to it, all God seems to have wanted all this time is for us to believe that He is, and to believe what He says.

Believing that the Bible says, By Whose stripes, we were healed, won't get anybody healed!! Instead of simply saying that the Bible says that, why don't we begin "believing for"….what the Bible says? That's the part that will pass the acid test.

No plague shall come nigh thy dwelling!! There's a good one. Why can't we believe for that? No weapon formed against me shall prosper. You say you don't qualify for that loan? God is able to make all grace abound toward you that you have all sufficiency in all things, able to abound to every good work. Be not conformed to this world: but be transformed by the renewing of your mind, that ye may prove what is that good, and acceptable, and perfect, will of God. And all things, whatsoever ye shall ask in prayer, believing, ye shall receive. What things soever ye desire, when ye pray, believe that ye receive them, and ye shall have them. If two of you shall agree on earth as touching any thing that they shall ask, it shall be done for them of my Father which is in heaven. If you abide in Jesus, and His words abide in you, you shall ask what you will, and it shall be done unto you.

Oh no, it's that name it, and claim it…blab it, and grab it doctrine that so many denominations have taken such a firm stand against.

We need to grow up. We need to learn how to think the way God thinks, and talk the way God talks. Can we do that? Sure, read the book!! If you hang around God long enough, He will rub off on you. You'll walk the way He walks, and talk the way He talks. Yeah but, God sees the whole thing, the beginning and the end!! He knows what's going to happen. Yes, He does.

Consider this….through the promises….We, like God, can see the end from the beginning of our circumstances.

Jer. 29:11
For I know the thoughts that I think toward you, saith the LORD, thoughts of peace, and not of evil, to give you an expected end.

God's promises are given so that we can have an expected end. Now we, like God, can see the end from the beginning of our circumstances. Through the promises, we can know what the will of God is for His people. His exact will!! It is for us, the church, to prove what is that good, acceptable, and perfect will of God, through FAITH!! For the just shall live by FAITH. From FAITH to FAITH. From FAITH unto salvation, to FAITH as a way of life, believing for the promises to be fulfilled in our lives.

Check out Week-4, we're talking about God's knowledge….Exact Knowledge!! Knowledge that is focused and so exact, it qualifies to be a Truth. A Truth that is so exact, so focused, so True, that it qualifies to be a law!! God has established all the promises from the foundation of the world.

Heb. 4:3
For we which have believed do enter into rest, as he said, As I have sworn in my wrath, if they shall enter into my rest: although the works were finished from the foundation of the world.

(Read "Entering God's Rest" Week-5-Day-5)

There is much to be learned about The KINGDOM of GOD. The only way to do it is to become students of the Bible. I resisted that for so many years. But one day I was asked to write an article for a newsletter. Little did I know, I would spend the rest of my life writing, digging, searching and uncovering truth about God, and His Kingdom.

I love it. I wouldn't have it any other way.

Lk. 12:32
Fear not, little flock; for it is your Father's good pleasure to give you the kingdom.

■ ◻ ■ ◻ ■ ◻ ■ ◻ ■

Week-9
The Power of His Resurrection

Week-9-Days-1-5
The Power of His Resurrection:
Day-1. Poverty, Sickness, & Death. Deut. 28:15-19 & 28:58-61
Day-2. The Spirit of The Lord is Upon Me. Lk. 4:18-19
Day-3. Go Ye Into All the World. Mk. 16:15-20
Day-4. Exceeding Great and precious Promises. 2 Pet. 1:4
Day-5. Insider Information. 2 Pet. 1:4

●

Day - 1
"Poverty, Sickness & Death"
(Deuteronomy 28:15-19, 58-61)

Kingdom Seekers
WEEK 9 DAY 1
02-10-2014

Deut. 28:15-21
15. But it shall come to pass, if thou wilt not hearken unto the voice of the LORD thy God, to observe to do all his commandments and his statutes which I command thee this day; that all these curses shall come upon thee, and overtake thee:
16. Cursed shalt thou be in the city, and cursed shalt thou be in the field.
17. Cursed shall be thy basket and thy store.
18. Cursed shall be the fruit of thy body, and the fruit of thy land, the increase of thy kine, and the flocks of thy sheep.
19. Cursed shalt thou be when thou comest in, and cursed shalt thou be when thou goest out.
20. The LORD shall send upon thee cursing, vexation, and rebuke, in all that thou settest thine hand unto for to do, until thou be destroyed, and until thou perish quickly; because of the wickedness of thy doings, whereby thou hast forsaken me.
21. The LORD shall make the pestilence cleave unto thee, until he have consumed thee from off the land, whither thou goest to possess it.

Cursed, cursed, cursed!! Cursed in the city and field, no matter where you're at. Cursed are your provisions and storehouse. cursed is the fruit of the body, the land, the animals. Cursed coming in, and going out. Cursed is whatever you set your hand to for to do, till you die!! Wow!!

But that's not all.

Deut. 28:58-61
58. If thou wilt not observe to do all the words of this law that are written in this book, that thou mayest fear this glorious and fearful name, THE LORD THY GOD;
59. Then the LORD will make thy plagues wonderful, and the plagues of thy seed, even great plagues, and of long continuance, and sore sicknesses, and of long continuance.
60. Moreover he will bring upon thee all the diseases of Egypt, which thou wast afraid of; and they shall cleave unto thee.
61. Also every sickness, and every plague, which is not written in the book of this law, them will the LORD bring upon thee, until thou be destroyed.

All manner of sickness and disease, even sicknesses and diseases not written in the book of the law, will come upon us.

That's OT truth. In just three words, the curse of the law is simply this, Poverty, Sickness, and Death.

NT truth,
Gal. 3:13
Christ hath redeemed us from the curse of the law, being made a curse for us: for it is written, Cursed is every one that hangeth on a tree:

We have been redeemed from the curse of the law. We are not under the curse of the law. Where no law is, there is no transgression.

The devil is a usurper, he will try to put sickness and disease on us but he has no authority to do so. The Truth will make our symptoms go away,…healing us. However, if we buy the symptoms with the ignorant and, or stupid words of our own mouths, we'll go through the whole process of the sickness or disease, even unto death, if that's the natural course of the symptoms.

Gal. 3:1-17
1. O foolish Galatians, who hath bewitched you, that ye should not obey the truth, before whose eyes Jesus Christ hath been evidently set forth, crucified among you?
2. This only would I learn of you, Received ye the Spirit by the works of the law, or by the hearing of faith?
3. Are ye so foolish? having begun in the Spirit, are ye now made perfect by the flesh?
4. Have ye suffered so many things in vain? if it be yet in vain.
5. He therefore that ministereth to you the Spirit, and worketh miracles among you, doeth he it by the works of the law, or by the hearing of faith?
6. Even as Abraham believed God, and it was accounted to him for righteousness.

7. Know ye therefore that they which are of faith, the same are the children of Abraham.

8. And the scripture, foreseeing that God would justify the heathen through faith, preached before the gospel unto Abraham, saying, In thee shall all nations be blessed.

9. So then they which be of faith are blessed with faithful Abraham.

10. For as many as are of the works of the law are under the curse: for it is written, Cursed is every one that continueth not in all things which are written in the book of the law to do them.

11. But that no man is justified by the law in the sight of God, it is evident: for, The just shall live by faith.

12. And the law is not of faith: but, The man that doeth them shall live in them.

13. Christ hath redeemed us from the curse of the law, being made a curse for us: for it is written, Cursed is every one that hangeth on a tree:

14. That the blessing of Abraham might come on the Gentiles through Jesus Christ; that we might receive the promise of the Spirit through faith.

15. Brethren, I speak after the manner of men; Though it be but a man's covenant, yet if it be confirmed, no man disannulleth, or addeth thereto.

16. Now to Abraham and his seed were the promises made. He saith not, And to seeds, as of many; but as of one, And to thy seed, which is Christ.

17. And this I say, that the covenant, that was confirmed before of God in Christ, the law, which was four hundred and thirty years after, cannot disannul, that it should make the promise of none effect.

(v.10) For as many as are of the works of the law are under the curse: for it is written, Cursed is every one that continueth not in all things which are written in the book of the law to do them.

If we innocently go back under the law, touch not, taste not, handle not, we inadvertently place ourselves back under the curse of the law.

Remember in
Gal. 4:3
Even so we, when we were children, were in bondage under the elements of the world.

When we were infants in Christ, we were still subject to the elements of the world. As we grow in the knowledge of Christ, we should be learning how to stand against the wiles of the devil, and after having done all to stand, stand therefore!! And win!!

Church, you don't have to put up with sickness, disease, aches, pains, or discomforts of any kind. It should be that it is impossible for us to succumb to any symptoms at all, but if we don't know who we are in Christ, well…the curse of the law is still out there. Though we are no longer subject to it, we will succumb to it through ignorance of the Truth of the Word.

• •

Day - 2
"The Spirit of The Lord is Upon Me"
(Luke 4:18-19)

Kingdom Seekers
WEEK 9 DAY 2
02-11-2014

Lk. 4:18-19
18. The Spirit of the Lord is upon me, because he hath anointed me to preach the gospel to the poor; he hath sent me to heal the brokenhearted, to preach deliverance to the captives, and recovering of sight to the blind, to set at liberty them that are bruised,
19. To preach the acceptable year of the Lord.

Do you remember Week-2-Days-1, 2, and 3, Week-3-Days-1, 2, and 3, Week-4-Days-2, 3, 4, and 5, Week-5-Days-2, 3, 4, and 5, Week-6-Days-1, 2, 3, and 4, Week-7-Days-1, 2, 3, and 4, and Week-8-Days-2, 3, 4, and 5? All these messages are to bring us to this point…. "The Spirit of the Lord is upon me."

Jesus physically, is not here. His body is, that's us, and we have all the gifts operating on the earth as the Spirit wills. No one man has all the gifts like Jesus did, but collectively, we have all the gifts in operation today. WE ARE TO GROW UP IN CHRIST!! Unto the stature of the fullness of Christ, ministering both to the body and to the heathen, the power of God to preach the gospel to the poor, to heal the brokenhearted, to preach deliverance to the captives, and recovering of sight to the blind, and to set at liberty them that are bruised, to preach the acceptable year of the Lord.

We all have gifts and callings. This whole Bible study is designed to bring the reader to the point of ministering on the earth just as Jesus did. Individually, as you are gifted, collectively, as the body of Christ, on the earth with all the gifts in operation. As we have seen in this Bible study, everything, EVERYTHING is done by Words.

In The KINGDOM of GOD, it's Words only!! The sword of the Spirit is not a metal sword, it is "The Word of God."

It is the Word on deliverance that will bring deliverance. It is the Word on recovery that will bring recovering. It is the Word on liberty that will produce liberty.

Don't you see it by now? Our words, spoken in The KINGDOM, will produce whatsoever we say….if we "believe" what we say!! If we "intend," what we say, if we "mean," what we say, if we "expect what we say shall surely come to pass." Then and only then, will we have what we said!!

Got it? We will live forever by our words. We can start now, today, this day, if you believe.

What did Jesus, have that we don't have on the earth? He had the Spirit of God in Him…you have the Spirit of God in you! He had God's Word to work with…you have the Word of God to work with! The centurion saw that He was a man under authority…you are a man or woman under authority! He had God's name…you have God's name!

He was God in the flesh…He was not here as God, He was here as a man, otherwise the plan of redemption would not have been legal. Adam was a man overthrown by a spiritual being, it had to be a man, to overthrow the spiritual being in order to be right and proper, and legal to achieve the desired result, everlasting life for those who believe.

2 Co. 3:18
But we all, with open face beholding as in a glass the glory of the Lord, are changed into the same image from glory to glory, even as by the Spirit of the Lord.

As we said before, the Bible is like a mirror, but it doesn't show us how we are. It shows us as God sees us, and we are changed into the image of what we see in the Word.

Gal. 2:19-20
19. For I through the law am dead to the law, that I might live unto God.
20. I am crucified with Christ: nevertheless I live; yet not I, but Christ liveth in me: and the life which I now live in the flesh I live by the faith of the Son of God, who loved me, and gave himself for me.

Jesus is our example.

Eph. 2:10
For we are his workmanship, created in Christ Jesus unto good works, which God hath before ordained that we should walk in them.

We are supposed to have the same ministry as Jesus had.

Jo. 14:12
Verily, verily, I say unto you, He that believeth on me, the works that I do shall he do also; and greater works than these shall he do; because I go unto my Father.

You may never raise a dead body back to life again, but when you witness Jesus to someone, and they receive Him as saviour, you have just raised a dead spirit into eternal life. In His earthly ministry, Jesus never did that.

Ro. 6:3-5
3. Know ye not, that so many of us as were baptized into Jesus Christ were baptized into his death?
4. Therefore we are buried with him by baptism into death: that like as Christ was raised up

from the dead by the glory of the Father, even so we also should walk in newness of life.

5. For if we have been planted together in the likeness of his death, we shall be also in the likeness of his resurrection:

I asked the question before. What resurrection? The actual, (death, burial, and resurrection) or the similitude (water baptism)?

You know, it really doesn't matter. Jesus is the same both then and now. He did no ministry before He was baptized. Let me repeat…He did no ministry before He was baptized!! His ministry today is exactly the same ministry He conducted, after water baptism.

We should walk in the same newness of life, as we grow in the knowledge of Him.

Lk. 12:32
Fear not, little flock; for it is your Father's good pleasure to give you the kingdom.

●●●

Day - 3
"Go Ye Into All the World"
(Mark 16:15-20)

Kingdom Seekers
WEEK 9 DAY 3
02-12-2014

Mk. 16:15-20
And he said unto them, Go ye into all the world, and preach the gospel to every creature.
16. He that believeth and is baptized shall be saved; but he that believeth not shall be damned.
17. And these signs shall follow them that believe; In my name shall they cast out devils; they shall speak with new tongues;
18. They shall take up serpents; and if they drink any deadly thing, it shall not hurt them; they shall lay hands on the sick, and they shall recover.
19. So then after the Lord had spoken unto them, he was received up into heaven, and sat on the right hand of God.
20. And they went forth, and preached every where, the Lord working with them, and confirming the word with signs following. Amen.

Go ye into all the world…   The great commission.
In my name shall they…   He gave us His name.

This is not the only place, but it is one of the places where Jesus gave us His name to use, IN MY NAME....

Mt. 24:14
And this gospel of the kingdom shall be preached in all the world for a witness unto all nations; and then shall the end come.

Today we're getting messages like, "Your inner man, Walk worthy of the Lord, Greater is He that is in you." Some of the messages we're getting are very powerful, moving, and exciting, but they don't seem to be able to get us on the other side of the learning curve. Please understand, I'm not trying to take away from this kind of message. We need to know as much as we can find out about God, and Bible teachings and examples.

Since going to my second Bible School, I've been preoccupied with the gospel of The KING-DOM. Why, I'm not sure, but I have studied nothing else since then. Knowing what the Bible says is important, but knowing how to use what the Bible says is whole different thing. A different concept. A different application. A right, a privilege, a way of living life in the Kingdom of God. Not just hearing about it...living it!!

Church is not like going to a movie. When we go to a movie, we don't expect to live out what we saw in the movie. We went there for entertainment, not to change our lifestyle. If we want to change our life style, we go to a tech school. We learn how to be a book keeper, florist or auto mechanic.

When we go to church, we should do it with the attitude of learning how to live life as a Christian, yes, but more importantly, as a citizen of a different kingdom, The KINGDOM of GOD. We live life differently here.

1 Co. 2:4-7
4. And my speech and my preaching was not with enticing words of man's wisdom, but in demonstration of the Spirit and of power:
5. That your faith should not stand in the wisdom of men, but in the power of God.
6. Howbeit we speak wisdom among them that are perfect: yet not the wisdom of this world, nor of the princes of this world, that come to nought:
7. But we speak the wisdom of God in a mystery, even the hidden wisdom, which God ordained before the world unto our glory:

Once we've tasted of the good Word of God, and of the powers of the world to come, there's no way that we would go back to living like the world does. Our old life is finished!!

Heb. 6:4-6
4. For it is impossible for those who were once enlightened, and have tasted of the heavenly gift, and were made partakers of the Holy Ghost,
5. And have tasted the good word of God, and the powers of the world to come,

6. If they shall fall away.

1 Tim. 4:12-16
12. Let no man despise thy youth; but be thou an example of the believers, in word, in conversation, in charity, in spirit, in faith, in purity.
13. Till I come, give attendance to reading, to exhortation, to doctrine.
14. Neglect not the gift that is in thee, which was given thee by prophecy, with the laying on of the hands of the presbytery.
15. Meditate upon these things; give thyself wholly to them; that thy profiting may appear to all.
16. Take heed unto thyself, and unto the doctrine; continue in them: for in doing this thou shalt both save thyself, and them that hear thee.

I know that Paul is writing to Timothy, and saying. I'm not coming to see you, but God is speaking to you today through me, and you really should give attendance to reading, to exhortation, to doctrine, that thy profiting may appear to all. You are a Christian, read of all men. An open book.

I shocked an audience once when I said, you haven't been ripped off, till you have been ripped off by a Christian!! Do you know why? Because you were not expecting it, not from a Christian!!

You don't see that in other religions.

Godliness is measured, good or bad, by the way Christians behave. That's Ok, they examined Jesus and made plenty of accusations against Him, but ultimately found no fault in Him. They just wanted Him out of the way. Are not His brothers and sisters here with us? Who does He think He is? He has made Himself as the Son of God.   CRUCIFY HIM!!

●●●●

Day - 4
"Exceeding Great and Precious Promises"
(II Peter 1:4)

Kingdom Seekers
WEEK 9 DAY 4
02-13-2014

2 Pet. 1:3-4
3. According as his divine power hath given unto us all things that pertain unto life and godliness, through the knowledge of him that hath called us to glory and virtue:
4. Whereby are given unto us exceeding great and precious promises: that by these ye might be partakers of the divine nature, having escaped the corruption that is in the world through lust.

We have talked about these before, but let's take another look at them.

Mt. 17:20
And Jesus said unto them, Because of your unbelief: for verily I say unto you, If ye have faith as a grain of mustard seed, ye shall say unto this mountain, Remove hence to yonder place; and it shall remove; and nothing shall be impossible unto you.

I know the context of the statement, "Because of your unbelief" but I also know the context of the statement, "and nothing shall be impossible unto you." This is the first insight on Kingdom rule, on the earth. "Because of your unbelief" had to do with their ministry. "If ye have faith as a grain of mustard seed, ye shall say unto this mountain, Remove hence to yonder place; and it shall remove; and nothing shall be impossible unto you." has to do with living according to KINGDOM RULE on the earth.

Mt. 18:18-20
18. Verily I say unto you, Whatsoever ye shall bind on earth shall be bound in heaven: and whatsoever ye shall loose on earth shall be loosed in heaven.
19. Again I say unto you, That if two of you shall agree on earth as touching any thing that they shall ask, it shall be done for them of my Father which is in heaven. (another insight on Kingdom rule on the earth)
20. For where two or three are gathered together in my name, there am I in the midst of them.

(When we use scripture in our agreement, that brings Jesus in on our agreement. He is scripture, He will agree with us and carry out the agreement.) If…we're believing "for" what we agreed on!!

Mt. 21:21-22
21. Verily I say unto you, If ye have faith, and doubt not, ye shall not only do this which is done to the fig tree, but also if ye shall say unto this mountain, Be thou removed, and be thou cast into the sea; it shall be done.
22. And all things, whatsoever ye shall ask in prayer, believing, ye shall receive.

Oh Wow! What a nice house, when did you move in? …two weeks ago. Oh, when did you buy it, and how much did it cost? We bought it three months ago at the prayer meeting without money and without price. When the time came for the manifestation, the money was there, waiting for us.

How do you explain that? I don't know, how do you explain how a seed grows?

Mk. 11:23-24
23. For verily I say unto you, That whosoever shall say unto this mountain, Be thou removed, and be thou cast into the sea; and shall not doubt in his heart, but shall believe that those things which he saith shall come to pass; he shall have whatsoever he saith.
24. Therefore I say unto you, What things soever ye desire, when ye pray, believe that ye receive them, and ye shall have them.

We receive (when we pray) not when the manifestation comes.

Lk. 17:6
And the Lord said, If ye had faith as a grain of mustard seed, ye might say unto this sycamine tree, Be thou plucked up by the root, and be thou planted in the sea; and it should obey you.

All things are done by the Word of His power!!

Jo. 14:13-14
13. And whatsoever ye shall ask in my name, that will I do, that the Father may be glorified in the Son.
14. If ye shall ask any thing in my name, I will do it.

This is the Word, speaking….I WILL DO IT!!

Jo. 15:7
If ye abide in me, and my words abide in you, ye shall ask what ye will, and it shall be done unto you.

What do you want in life? Ask God for it, believe you receive it when you pray, it shall be done unto you!!

Jo. 15:5
I am the vine, ye are the branches: He that abideth in me, and I in him, the same bringeth forth much fruit: for without me ye can do nothing.

Without Words, The KINGDOM of GOD would be dysfunctional. It just wouldn't work. Words are needed to describe what we want, then the manifestation comes to pass, and then we see the manifestation. Once we know how the system works, we can work the system.

1 Jo. 5:14-15
14. And this is the confidence that we have in him, that, if we ask any thing according to his will, he heareth us:
15. And if we know that he hear us, whatsoever we ask, we know that we have the petitions that we desired of him.

A most excellent place to start is "the promises." The promises of God in the Bible, are God's will for His people!

Lk. 12:32
Fear not, little flock; it is your Father's good pleasure to give you the kingdom.

• • • • •

Day - 5
"Insider Information"
(II Peter 1:4)

Kingdom Seekers
WEEK 9 DAY 5
02-14-2014

Jo. 15:18-20
18. If the world hate you, ye know that it hated me before it hated you.
19. If ye were of the world, the world would love his own: but because ye are not of the world, but I have chosen you out of the world, therefore the world hateth you.
20. Remember the word that I said unto you, The servant is not greater than his lord. If they have persecuted me, they will also persecute you; if they have kept my saying, they will keep yours also.

As we've seen in earlier messages, we live in a closed society. One cannot receive Jesus, except God reveals Him. One cannot come to God, except Jesus reveals Him. We are chosen out of the world. As we grow in the knowledge of Him, we are given "inside information" on how things are done in the spirit, and the life.

Jo. 14:6
I am the way, the truth, and the life: no man cometh unto the Father, but by me.

Closed society.

Jo. 6:63
It is the spirit that quickeneth; the flesh profiteth nothing: the words that I speak unto you, they are spirit, and they are life.

Jesus didn't talk the way the world talked, although He did say things in ministry like, A sower went out to sow…a man found a treasure in a field…a woman lost a coin…a woman put leaven in a lump… Jesus did that to illustrate a spiritual truth.

Ro. 12:2
And be not conformed to this world: but be ye transformed by the renewing of your mind, that ye may prove what is that good, and acceptable, and perfect, will of God.

Through the promises of God recorded in the Bible, we…like God, can see the end from the beginning of our circumstances. Through these promises, we know what the will of God is for His people.

1 Jo. 5:13-15

13. These things have I written unto you that believe on the name of the Son of God; that ye may know that ye have eternal life, and that ye may believe on the name of the Son of God.

14. And this is the confidence that we have in him, that, if we ask any thing according to his will, he heareth us:

15. And if we know that he hear us, whatsoever we ask, we know that we have the petitions that we desired of him.

What is the will of God for us? Well we can certainly start with the promises and work from there.

1 Co. 2:9-12

9. But as it is written, Eye hath not seen, nor ear heard, neither have entered into the heart of man, the things which God hath prepared for them that love him.

10. But God hath revealed them unto us by his Spirit: for the Spirit searcheth all things, yea, the deep things of God.

11. For what man knoweth the things of a man, save the spirit of man which is in him? even so the things of God knoweth no man, but the Spirit of God.

12. Now we have received, not the spirit of the world, but the spirit which is of God; that we might know the things that are freely given to us of God.

Did you catch that? God has revealed them unto us by His Spirit!!

The biggest part of my ministry is teaching people stuff that they already know. The things I'm sharing with you, you already know, but it may not have been real to you. You may not have seen it this way before. You may not have "measured" it as a help, before.

Mk. 4:21-25

21. And he said unto them, Is a candle brought to be put under a bushel, or under a bed? and not to be set on a candlestick?

22. For there is nothing hid, which shall not be manifested; neither was any thing kept secret, but that it should come abroad.

23. If any man have ears to hear, let him hear.

24. And he said unto them, Take heed what ye hear: with what measure ye mete, it shall be measured to you: and unto you that hear shall more be given.

25. For he that hath, to him shall be given: and he that hath not, from him shall be taken even that which he hath.

In the world, insider information will put you in jail in a heartbeat, but in The KINGDOM of GOD, insider information is a privilege and a blessing that we have of God, so that we can live out our lives according to KINGDOM RULE, in the peace that passes understanding, in confidence, on the earth, in the here and now! Rights and privileges for the children of the Most High God.

There are things that accompany Righteousness, and Righteousness has been restored. While we were yet sinners, Christ died for us. Sin is no longer imputed to us because of the Righteousness of God which has been given to us who believe.

When sickness comes, we know the answer, Himself took my infirmities and bare my sicknesses, and by His stripes, we were healed! The symptoms are real, but we just called those things that are not as though they were. NOW, healing can move in and take place. How? By Jesus confirming the "Word," with signs following.

And it didn't cost a dime!! How cool is that?

Psa. 23:5
Thou preparest a table before me in the presence of mine enemies: thou anointest my head with oil; my cup runneth over.

Divine health is on the table... do you want in?

Lk. 12:32
Fear not little flock, for it is your Father's good pleasure to give you the Kingdom.

■ ◻ ■ ◻ ■ ◻ ■ ◻ ■ ◻ ■ ◻

Week-10
Building on the Rock

Week-10-Days-1-5
Building on the Rock:
Day-1. The Parable of The Two Builders. Mt. 7:24-27
Day-2. Bits and Rudders. Jas. 3:2-4
Day-3. Servants and disciples. Mt. 10:24-25
Day-4. A Solid Foundation. 1 Co. 3:9-17
Day-5. A Hostile Takeover. Gen. 11:1-9

●

Day - 1
"The Parable of The Two Builders"
(Matthews 7:24-27)

Kingdom Seekers
WEEK 10 DAY 1
02-17-2014

Mt. 7:24-27
24. Therefore whosoever heareth these sayings of mine, and doeth them, I will liken him unto a wise man, which built his house upon a rock:
25. And the rain descended, and the floods came, and the winds blew, and beat upon that house; and it fell not: for it was founded upon a rock.
26. And every one that heareth these sayings of mine, and doeth them not, shall be likened unto a foolish man, which built his house upon the sand:
27. And the rain descended, and the floods came, and the winds blew, and beat upon that house; and it fell: and great was the fall of it.

For many years, I thought that Jesus was talking about a saved person and an unsaved person. This is not true. They are both saved, both love God, and both have the same opportunity to succeed in life, as the other. One heard the Word, and did it… the other heard the same Word, but didn't do it.

Jas. 1:22-25

22. But be ye doers of the word, and not hearers only, deceiving your own selves.

23. For if any be a hearer of the word, and not a doer, he is like unto a man beholding his natural face in a glass:

24. For he beholdeth himself, and goeth his way, and straightway forgetteth what manner of man he was.

25. But whoso looketh into the perfect law of liberty, and continueth therein, he being not a forgetful hearer, but a doer of the work, this man shall be blessed in his deed.

Many are hearers, but not doers. They don't see the promises as the answers to our needs, or how to activate them.

Read on in
Jas. 1:26
If any man among you seem to be religious, and bridleth not his tongue, but deceiveth his own heart, this man's religion is vain.

As I have said many times before, it's all about "words," in The KINGDOM of GOD. We need to learn how to talk like God talks, and think like God thinks. Until we receive our expected end. (The expected end, being the manifestation of the promise you are believing for.)

Jer. 29:11
For I know the thoughts that I think toward you, saith the LORD, thoughts of peace, and not of evil, to give you an expected end.

God set it all up before the foundation of the world.

Heb. 4:3-4
3. For we which have believed do enter into rest, as he said, As I have sworn in my wrath, if they shall enter into my rest: although the works were finished from the foundation of the world.

4. For he spake in a certain place of the seventh day on this wise, And God did rest the seventh day from all his works.

Heb. 4:9-10
9. There remaineth therefore a rest to the people of God.
10. For he that is entered into his rest, he also hath ceased from his own works, as God did from his.

If you believe "Himself took our infirmities, and bare our sicknesses" is in the Bible, that doesn't mean you're going to be healed. If you believe that "Himself took our infirmities, and bare our sicknesses" is designed to effect a healing for you, but if you don't act on it, you're still not going to get healed.

There's only one way to activate a promise of God in your life. You need to speak it, doubt not in your heart that it will actually happen, then believe what you said shall indeed happen. Jesus said, for anyone who does that, they will have what they said!!

Let me reiterate. Find a promise that covers your need, speak it, doubt not in your heart, but believe what you said shall come to pass. Oh, is that how it works? Yes, that's how it works!!

We are created beings. Created in God's image and after His likeness. We are born-again "in Him," with full rights and privileges of the Righteousness that God has provided for us, for justification of eternal life.

A moment ago I said, we are created beings. Let me take it a step further. We are creative beings too.

Where there is no way, God has given us a way.

Remember, in this Bible study, we are talking about who Jesus was before He was Jesus. He was "The Word of God!!" In Jo.14:6. Jesus said, "I am the way, the truth, and the life..."

WORDS!! Words are the way of life in The KINGDOM of GOD. We don't have pencils, typewriters, or computers available to us, we don't have hammers, drills, or screwdrivers. We don't have road graders, front loaders, or any type of heavy equipment. No money, no gold, no silver. It's words only in The KINGDOM of GOD.

Remember, the Word, dwells in you now. He knows if you're believing for what you just said, or not. He is a discerner of the thoughts and intents of our hearts. We can't fool Him, He knows if we're believing for what we said, or not. If not...He's not obligated to confirm the Word with signs following. In case you haven't noticed, He will help when we're believing for Him to help, but He doesn't help when we're not believing for Him to help. We've had some successes and some failures, haven't we.

Lk. 12:32
Fear not, little flock; for it is your Father's good pleasure to give you the kingdom.

••

Day - 2
"Bits and Rudders"
(James 3:2-4)

Kingdom Seekers
WEEK 10 DAY 2
02-18-2014

Jas. 3:1-4
1. My brethren, be not many masters, knowing that we shall receive the greater condemnation.
2. For in many things we offend all. If any man offend not in word, the same is a perfect man, and able also to bridle the whole body.
3. Behold, we put bits in the horses' mouths, that they may obey us; and we turn about their whole body.
4. Behold also the ships, which though they be so great, and are driven of fierce winds, yet are they turned about with a very small helm, whithersoever the governor listeth.

Okay, we're coming down to the wire on this Bible study. If you just joined us, you might find yourself at a loss because you really need to start at the beginning in order to understand what's going on in these last three weeks. This is where the rubber meets the road. In fact the rubber met the road some time back, we're just cruising now gathering a little more information as we go.

The rubber I spoke of is not tire rubber. It is the soles of our shoes. We are on a highway called "The Way of Holiness." you'll find it in.

Isa. 35:8-10
8. And an highway shall be there, and a way, and it shall be called The way of holiness; the unclean shall not pass over it; but it shall be for those: the wayfaring men, though fools, shall not err therein.
9. No lion shall be there, nor any ravenous beast shall go up thereon, it shall not be found there; but the redeemed shall walk there:
10. And the ransomed of the LORD shall return, and come to Zion with songs and everlasting joy upon their heads: they shall obtain joy and gladness, and sorrow and sighing shall flee away.

It is the "way" that John built. That is to say...John the Baptist.

Isa. 40:3-4
3. The voice of him that crieth in the wilderness, Prepare ye the way of the LORD, make straight in the desert a highway for our God.
4. Every valley shall be exalted, and every mountain and hill shall be made low: and the crooked

shall be made straight, and the rough places plain:

We will discuss this in more detail in Week-11-Day-5, but for now, let's just say that we don't have to go to Jerusalem to pray. We don't have to go to our local church building to speak to the Lord, or have someone else pray for us in our stead. We are told to come boldly to the Throne of Grace, and find help in time of need.

Hey, on this road, the high places have been brought down low. The low places have been raised up and the crooked places made straight and the rough places made plain.

If you have a problem, you take care of it using the Word of God, YOU steer your way through the problem and overcome the problem with the Word!! You know the one. The one that God released in Genesis. The discerner of the thoughts and intents of the heart. The creative power of God. The Word, that performs the doing of everything that God says.

The one that said in
Jo. 14:13-14
13. And whatsoever ye shall ask in my name, that will I do, that the Father may be glorified in the Son.
14. If ye shall ask any thing in my name, I will do it.

You are in charge, whether you realize it or not, feel like it or not, or even want to be or not, you are in charge of your life.

Php. 2:13
For it is God which worketh in you both to will and to do of his good pleasure.

Ro. 12:2
And be not conformed to this world: but be ye transformed by the renewing of your mind, that ye may prove what is that good, and acceptable, and perfect, will of God.

God is not going to prove what is the good, acceptable, and perfect will of God in your life!!! He told you to do that!!! Your tongue is the bit in your mouth. Your tongue is the rudder that navigates the course of your life on planet earth. If you have a problem, chances are it was your own words that put you there. You are living, in the sum of your words, right now. We are all a product of what we've been taught. We need to get serious and learn how to talk the way God talks, and do things the way God does things.

Re-read Week-5-Day-5. "Entering God's Rest."

Heb. 3:7-11
7. Wherefore as the Holy Ghost saith, To day if ye will hear his voice,
8. Harden not your hearts, as in the provocation, in the day of temptation in the wilderness:

9. When your fathers tempted me, proved me, and saw my works forty years.

10. Wherefore I was grieved with that generation, and said, They do alway err in their heart; and they have not known my ways.

11. So I sware in my wrath, They shall not enter into my rest.

You are in charge of your life. If you knew it...things would be different...wouldn't they? Yes...indeed!!

Old familiar scripture is only now taking on a new dimension and meaning when seen from The "KINGDOM perspective."

Lk. 12:32
Fear not, little flock; for it is your Father's good pleasure to give you the kingdom.

●●●

Day - 3
"Servants and Disciples"
(Matthew 10:24-25)

Kingdom Seekers
WEEK 10 DAY 3
02-19-2014

Mt. 10:24-25
24. The disciple is not above his master, nor the servant above his lord.

25. It is enough for the disciple that he be as his master, and the servant as his lord. If they have called the master of the house Beelzebub, how much more shall they call them of his household?

This is the spot that Kingdom Seekers, has been bringing us to all along. It is enough that the disciple be AS his Master, and the Servant AS his Lord. Jesus has been teaching us, training us, and preparing us to rule in life just AS He would if He were here in the flesh.

Do you remember Week-2-Day-2? "Righteousness speaks"

Ro. 10:6-10
6. But the righteousness which is of faith speaketh on this wise, Say not in thine heart, Who shall ascend into heaven? (that is, to bring Christ down from above:)

7. Or, Who shall descend into the deep? (that is, to bring up Christ again from the dead.)

8. But what saith it? The word is nigh thee, even in thy mouth, and in thy heart: that is, the word of faith, which we preach;

9. That if thou shalt confess with thy mouth the Lord Jesus, and shalt believe in thine heart that

God hath raised him from the dead, thou shalt be saved.

10. For with the heart man believeth unto righteousness; and with the mouth confession is made unto salvation.

Well really, from Week-2 through Week-9. All of it!!

Php. 2:5-6
5. Let this mind be in you, which was also in Christ Jesus:
6. Who, being in the form of God, thought it not robbery to be equal with God:

1 Co. 2:16
For who hath known the mind of the Lord, that he may instruct him? But we have the mind of Christ.

Don't be thinking that you are some helpless wimp that the devil can bowl over and devour at his will!! You are a child of the Most High God, with rights and privileges, and Righteousness Speaks!

That road that John built, no low spots, no high spots, straight, and smooth. We don't have to go to Jerusalem to pray, we don't have to call Jesus in on the scene to help us out of this mess, the Word is nigh thee, even in thy mouth and in thy heart, the Word of Faith which we preach!! Now that you've been enlightened, now that you've tasted of the good Word of God, don't be too easily removed from the simplicity of the gospel.

Jesus is teaching us, if you have a problem, you are to take care of it; you have My Word, My Spirit, and My Name. you deal with your own problems just AS I would, if I were here…And whatsoever ye shall ask in my name, THAT WILL I DO, that the Father may be glorified in the Son. If ye shall ask any thing in my name, I WILL DO IT.

Look at it this way, everything that God said in Genesis, the Word, performed the doing of what was said. The Word was made flesh, we now call the Word, Jesus. Jesus is saying, yes, I do all that God says, and now, I will do what YOU say, IN MY NAME!!

There is a qualifier here, our Words need to be filled with intent. Our Words need to be accompanied with thought and purpose, directed and articulated to produce a desired result. Because the Word of God is in you, He is a discerner of the thoughts and intents of the heart. We need to learn how to rule on the earth with our Words, it's Words only in The KINGDOM of GOD. It will take a while, but the blessing is that we can start now, today.

I've been studying The KINGDOM of GOD since April, of 2008. I know the date because it was a class project in a Bible School I was attending at the time. There is so much to be learned, so much to share.

Bible teachings and doctrine seem to be a standard apart from Kingdom teaching. The Bible teaches Faith and Righteousness as a standard unto itself, but when you see these teachings from

The KINGDOM perspective, it takes on a whole new dimension. From the Bible perspective, we're seeing Bible truth, but not really getting involved as a participant. From The KINGDOM perspective, we become very much involved, it becomes a way of life for us to live out.

I've never mentioned this before, but you may have noticed, I never read these writings before I post them. I don't consider myself a writer or an author, but I did hear something one day that I use in my writing. It was said that if I had a writer's block, I should just spit it out, and clean it up later. These writings are from the heart. When I put them in book form, I'll clean them up. For now, you get what you get. Okay?

Some of you, I know. Some of you, I'll never meet in this lifetime, never even know that you followed the Kingdom Seekers Bible study at all, but I want you to know that I love you all. My hope is that this study will improve the lives of everyone who reads it.

Lk. 12:32
Fear not, little flock; for it is your Father's good pleasure to give you the kingdom.

●●●●

Day - 4
"A Solid Foundation"
(I Corinthians 3:9-17)

Kingdom Seekers
WEEK 10 DAY 4
02-20-2014

1 Co. 3:9-11
9. For we are labourers together with God: ye are God's husbandry, ye are God's building.
10. According to the grace of God which is given unto me, as a wise masterbuilder, I have laid the foundation, and another buildeth thereon. But let every man take heed how he buildeth thereupon.
11. For other foundation can no man lay than that is laid, which is Jesus Christ.

In view of what we're studying in this Bible study, I would like to re-phrase verse 11 to read this way.

(v.11) For other foundation can no man lay than that is laid, which is "The Word of God."

Because that's who Jesus is, the manifested Word of God, in the flesh. I have a dear friend looking over a mini book I wrote recently called "The Word of God - Literally The Word." the book is based on *Heb.6:1a. Therefore leaving the principles of the doctrine of Christ, let us go on unto perfection…*

Who knows how many times we read over that scripture and don't realize what it is saying. Can you imagine that? Leaving the principles and doctrine of Christ? Whaaat?

She is having just as difficult a time as I did, distinguishing "the Word," from "Jesus." The Word is a Spiritual entity. The second person of the God Head. Was it Jesus that came and took upon Himself our sin, and died for us? YES!! But more importantly, it was The Word, made flesh, that did it. The Lamb slain before the foundation of the world. God didn't create some other being to do this. He sent His Word…to do it. Everything God does, He does it by using Words!!

Is God a man that He should lie? No!! He won't ever mislead us, He is Truth, He is Light, He is Love, our counselor, our healer, our justifier, our provider. He is anything and everything we need. Apart from Him, we can do nothing, not even exist.

In an earthly kingdom, the King is supported by the people. In GOD'S KINGDOM, the King supports the needs of people. How cool is that?… Very!!

Deut. 29:29
The secret things belong unto the LORD our God: but those things which are revealed belong unto us and to our children for ever, that we may do all the words of this law.

That's cool, right and proper, we don't need to know everything, but as pertaining to the issues of life, Jesus said,

Mk. 4:21-25
21. And he said unto them, Is a candle brought to be put under a bushel, or under a bed? and not to be set on a candlestick?
22. For there is nothing hid, which shall not be manifested; neither was any thing kept secret, but that it should come abroad.
23. If any man have ears to hear, let him hear.
24. And he said unto them, Take heed what ye hear: with what measure ye mete, it shall be measured to you: and unto you that hear shall more be given.
25. For he that hath, to him shall be given: and he that hath not, from him shall be taken even that which he hath.

If you're not living by the Word of God, you're living according to your first nature. The sin nature. Even if you are born-again. This situation comes under the category of being "a Carnal Christian."

Ro. 8:6
For to be carnally minded is death; but to be spiritually minded is life and peace.

This doesn't mean you're not saved, it just means that God is not going to overpower your free will and make you do something against your will, and He will let you "do it your way." To be carnally minded, is to be without God's help and influence in your life. You are saved, but you're not living the overcoming life that God has prepared for those who love Him. Jesus came to give us an abundant life. The only way to get there from here is to take God at His Word, a solid foundation to live by. We will live forever by His Word.

Mt. 4:4
It is written, Man shall not live by bread alone, but by every word that proceedeth out of the mouth of God.

Again, we are focusing in on the promises. The promises are God's will for His people. We can exercise confidence in His Word to us.

1 Jo. 5:13-15
13. These things have I written unto you that believe on the name of the Son of God; that ye may know that ye have eternal life, and that ye may believe on the name of the Son of God.
14. And this is the confidence that we have in him, that, if we ask any thing according to his will, he heareth us:
15. And if we know that he hear us, whatsoever we ask, we know that we have the petitions that we desired of him.

We are children of promise. Don't lean on your own understanding, lean on the promises, they are designed to "produce" what they promise. First the blade, then the ear, after that, the full corn in the ear. It's a process, as a man should cast seed into the ground. That seed will grow if we doubt not, but believe. All things are possible to them that believe.

Lk. 12:32
Fear not, little flock; for it is your Father's good pleasure to give you the kingdom.

● ● ● ● ●

Day - 5
"A Hostile Takeover"
(Genesis 11:1-9)

Kingdom Seekers
WEEK 10 DAY 5
02-21-2014

Point of reference,
Gen. 11:1-9
1. And the whole earth was of one language, and of one speech.

2. And it came to pass, as they journeyed from the east, that they found a plain in the land of Shinar; and they dwelt there.

3. And they said one to another, Go to, let us make brick, and burn them thoroughly. And they had brick for stone, and slime had they for mortar.

4. And they said, Go to, let us build us a city and a tower, whose top may reach unto heaven; and let us make us a name, lest we be scattered abroad upon the face of the whole earth.

5. And the LORD came down to see the city and the tower, which the children of men builded.

6. And the LORD said, Behold, the people is one, and they have all one language; and this they begin to do: and now nothing will be restrained from them, which they have imagined to do.

7. Go to, let us go down, and there confound their language, that they may not understand one another's speech.

8. So the LORD scattered them abroad from thence upon the face of all the earth: and they left off to build the city.

9. Therefore is the name of it called Babel; because the LORD did there confound the language of all the earth: and from thence did the LORD scatter them abroad upon the face of all the earth.

Principle verse,

(v.6)

And the LORD said, Behold, the people is one, and they have all one language; and this they begin to do: and now nothing will be restrained from them, which they have imagined to do.

Does the Bible teach "an hostile takeover"? No. that's been a problem in my ministry. I teach things that the Bible just doesn't say in so many words.

However, the Bible does say in

2 Co. 4:4

In whom the god of this world hath blinded the minds of them which believe not, lest the light of the glorious gospel of Christ, who is the image of God, should shine unto them.

The devil has blinded the minds of all mankind. My point is this, man never did lose dominion. What happened was that the devil overthrew man and took the top position of the dominion that God gave man, else verse 6 would not have been written.

Remember?

Heb. 4:3b

"...although the works were finished from the foundation of the world."

The plan of salvation was already in place.

Mt. 8:17

That it might be fulfilled which was spoken by Esaias the prophet, saying, Himself took our infirmities, and bare our sicknesses.

Was already stated, and established!

Mt. 18:19, agreement… Mk. 11:23… already established! "the Works" were finished from the foundation of the world!! (God confounded their language so that they could no longer agree.)

So what's my point? Man never did lose dominion. Spiritual Truth, Spiritual Law has been working all along, we just didn't know it. That's why we need to seek The KINGDOM of GOD, and His Righteousness. There are laws that govern The KINGDOM, and there are things that accompany Righteousness.

Hence, Kingdom Seekers Bible study. It is designed to bring the common Christian believer from a place of living a defeated lifestyle to a place of Spiritual maturity to where he or she can live out their life according to KINGDOM RULE while still on the earth.

God didn't save us, to take us. He saved us to be examples just like Jesus was. Oh, to know Him and the power of His resurrection. Jesus never "took" authority over anything. Jesus, simply exercised the authority He knew He had!!

We need to learn to do the same thing….because we can!!! Once the devil knows that we know who we are in Christ Jesus, he'll back off just like he did from Jesus. Of course that doesn't mean he won't try to come back.

Mk. 11:23 works both ways. What God gave us for a blessing, the devil has perverted it.

That's why witchcraft, black magic and all that other stuff works. Does it really work? Yes, it really works, but greater is He that is in us than he that is in the world. We are not subject to that stuff, neither indeed can be, IF we know who we are in Christ Jesus.

Let me clarify again, we don't have dominion over people. We only have dominion over the earth, the cattle, the foul, and every creeping thing on the earth. Everything in it, on it, and above it. Not your husband, or your wife, or anybody else!!!!! God doesn't even exercise control over us….but the devil does, or tries to.

We don't have to put up with the wiles of the devil, we have God's Word, His Name, and his Spirit. If God be for us, who can be against us?

Eph. 6:10-17
10. Finally, my brethren, be strong in the Lord, and in the power of his might.
11. Put on the whole armour of God, that ye may be able to stand against the wiles of the devil.
12. For we wrestle not against flesh and blood, but against principalities, against powers, against the rulers of the darkness of this world, against spiritual wickedness in high places.
13. Wherefore take unto you the whole armour of God, that ye may be able to withstand in the evil day, and having done all, to stand.

14. Stand therefore, having your loins girt about with truth, and having on the breastplate of righteousness;

15. And your feet shod with the preparation of the gospel of peace;

16. Above all, taking the shield of faith, wherewith ye shall be able to quench all the fiery darts of the wicked.

17. And take the helmet of salvation, and the sword of the Spirit, which is the word of God:

■ ◻ ■ ◻ ■ ◻ ■ ◻ ■ ◻ ■

Week-11
The Faith Walk of Today

Week-11-Days-1-5
The Faith Walk of Today:
Day-1. Faith by Works. Jas. 2:14-16
Day-2. A Hearing Heart. 1 Kgs. 3:5-9
Day-3. The Double Minded Man. Jas. 1:1-8
Day-4. Ambassadors For Christ. 2 Co. 5:20
Day-5. Entering God's Rest II. Heb. 3:10 and 4:16

●

Day - 1
"Faith by Works"
(James 2:14-16)

Kingdom Seekers
WEEK 11 DAY 1
02-24-2014

Jas. 2:14-17
14. What doth it profit, my brethren, though a man say he hath faith, and have not works? can faith save him?
15. If a brother or sister be naked, and destitute of daily food,
16. And one of you say unto them, Depart in peace, be ye warmed and filled; notwithstanding ye give them not those things which are needful to the body; what doth it profit?
17. Even so faith, if it hath not works, is dead, being alone.

Jesus used natural examples in His ministry, A sower went out to sow…a woman who lost a coin…. The Master of the house went on a long journey leaving his servants in charge…

Faith without works is dead, is not just a point of interest, it is a fact. A woman who is expecting a baby is not going to wait till the baby arrives to gather up small clothing and diapers feeding bottles. No, no, she will have them way ahead of time and be ready when the baby arrives. Whether it be of natural childbirth or adoption, she will see to it that she is ready for that baby when it comes.

It's the same when believing God for something. Prepare for it. As though you're expecting it to surely come to pass. Get ready, get ready, get ready. Why? Because if you're expecting it, it will surely be made manifest by Jesus confirming the Word, with signs following. It's coming….get ready!!

That being said…if you're not getting ready for it when it comes…Jesus is not obligated to produce it with signs following….is He!! You're not expecting, You're not in Faith, there are no works…you're not going to get anything!!

Jesus said in Jo. 14:13-14. That He would do whatsoever we ask in His name…RIGHT? So ask believing you receive as you're asking, and then get ready for it, for when it comes. Simple instruction, why is it so hard to do?

Jas. 2:17-26
17. Even so faith, if it hath not works, is dead, being alone.
18. Yea, a man may say, Thou hast faith, and I have works: show me thy faith without thy works, and I will show thee my faith by my works.
19. Thou believest that there is one God; thou doest well: the devils also believe, and tremble.
20. But wilt thou know, O vain man, that faith without works is dead?
21. Was not Abraham our father justified by works, when he had offered Isaac his son upon the altar?
22. Seest thou how faith wrought with his works, and by works was faith made perfect?
23. And the scripture was fulfilled which saith, Abraham believed God, and it was imputed unto him for righteousness: and he was called the Friend of God.
24. Ye see then how that by works a man is justified, and not by faith only.
25. Likewise also was not Rahab the harlot justified by works, when she had received the messengers, and had sent them out another way?
26. For as the body without the spirit is dead, so faith without works is dead also.

The thing is, we ask God for the things we want and or need, then we go on about our lives as always, "expecting"….nothing.

Heb. 2:1-4
1. Therefore we ought to give the more earnest heed to the things which we have heard, lest at any time we should let them slip.
2. For if the word spoken by angels was stedfast, and every transgression and disobedience received a just recompense of reward;
3. How shall we escape, if we neglect so great salvation; which at the first began to be spoken by the Lord, and was confirmed unto us by them that heard him;
4. God also bearing them witness, both with signs and wonders, and with divers miracles, and gifts of the Holy Ghost, according to his own will?

Verse 4 sounds a lot like
Mk. 16:20
And they went forth, and preached every where, the Lord working with them, and confirming

the word with signs following. Amen.

If you have asked God for a house or a car, it would follow that you would be thinking in terms of drapery's and carpeting, corner lot or acreage. If it's a car you're believing for, you should be thinking standard or automatic, two or four wheel drive. You should be collecting things like a the steering wheel cover you want, floor mats, tinted windows, or whatever…

Faith without works is dead. You have asked, but you're not preparing for it. You're not preparing because you're not "expecting." Yes, Faith is the substance of things hoped for, but you're not even hoping, you're just "wanting."

Jas. 1:2-8
2. My brethren, count it all joy when ye fall into divers temptations;
3. Knowing this, that the trying of your faith worketh patience.
4. But let patience have her perfect work, that ye may be perfect and entire, wanting nothing.
5. If any of you lack wisdom, let him ask of God, that giveth to all men liberally, and upbraideth not; and it shall be given him.
6. But let him ask in faith, nothing wavering. For he that wavereth is like a wave of the sea driven with the wind and tossed.
7. For let not that man think that he shall receive any thing of the Lord.
8. A double minded man is unstable in all his ways.

It is your Father's good pleasure to give you The KINGDOM.

●●

Day - 2
"A Hearing Heart"
(1 Kings 3:5-9)

Kingdom Seekers
WEEK 11 DAY 2
02-25-2014

1 Kgs. 3:5-9
5. In Gibeon the LORD appeared to Solomon in a dream by night: and God said, Ask what I shall give thee.
6. And Solomon said, Thou hast showed unto thy servant David my father great mercy, according as he walked before thee in truth, and in righteousness, and in uprightness of heart with thee; and thou hast kept for him this great kindness, that thou hast given him a son to sit on his throne, as it is this day.
7. And now, O LORD my God, thou hast made thy servant king instead of David my father:

and I am but a little child: I know not how to go out or come in.

8. And thy servant is in the midst of thy people which thou hast chosen, a great people, that cannot be numbered nor counted for multitude.

9. Give therefore thy servant an understanding heart to judge thy people, that I may discern between good and bad: for who is able to judge this thy so great a people?

You know, it doesn't take long talking to someone to know that they don't know what they're talking about.

Whether you're talking about horses or baseball, computer repair or hair styling, you can tell whether this person knows what they're talking about. Even if you yourself don't know that much about the subject of the conversation, you can tell pretty quick that this guy or that girl doesn't either.

I am currently having an exchange on facebook with a young lady in Africa. She is very hungry to learn about God, and the truth of His KINGDOM. She want's to know with all her heart, but I can tell, she doesn't know anything about The KINGDOM, or the laws and principles that govern The KINGDOM. She and I, and all of us…yes, all of us, need to pray to God for a hearing heart.

We can be told what to do and how to do it, but without understanding, knowledge is useless. So we need to pray for a hearing heart. A good example of what I'm sharing is this, with all the translations of the Bible that are out there, the Bible may as well still be written in Greek and Hebrew because if God doesn't reveal to you what you're reading, you're not going to know!!!

All I can do is tell her about The KINGDOM. It's up to God, to give her knowledge and understanding so that she can live according to KINGDOM RULE on the earth.

Eph. 1:15-21
15. Wherefore I also, after I heard of your faith in the Lord Jesus, and love unto all the saints,
16. Cease not to give thanks for you, making mention of you in my prayers;
17. That the God of our Lord Jesus Christ, the Father of glory, may give unto you the spirit of wisdom and revelation in the knowledge of him:
18. The eyes of your understanding being enlightened; that ye may know what is the hope of his calling, and what the riches of the glory of his inheritance in the saints,
19. And what is the exceeding greatness of his power to us-ward who believe, according to the working of his mighty power,
20. Which he wrought in Christ, when he raised him from the dead, and set him at his own right hand in the heavenly places,
21. Far above all principality, and power, and might, and dominion, and every name that is named, not only in this world, but also in that which is to come:

Col. 1:7-17
7. As ye also learned of Epaphras our dear fellowservant, who is for you a faithful minister of Christ;
8. Who also declared unto us your love in the Spirit.

9. For this cause we also, since the day we heard it, do not cease to pray for you, and to desire that ye might be filled with the knowledge of his will in all wisdom and spiritual understanding;

10. That ye might walk worthy of the Lord unto all pleasing, being fruitful in every good work, and increasing in the knowledge of God;

11. Strengthened with all might, according to his glorious power, unto all patience and longsuffering with joyfulness;

12. Giving thanks unto the Father, which hath made us meet to be partakers of the inheritance of the saints in light:

13. Who hath delivered us from the power of darkness, and hath translated us into the kingdom of his dear Son:

14. In whom we have redemption through his blood, even the forgiveness of sins:

15. Who is the image of the invisible God, the firstborn of every creature:

16. For by him were all things created, that are in heaven, and that are in earth, visible and invisible, whether they be thrones, or dominions, or principalities, or powers: all things were created by him, and for him:

17. And he is before all things, and by him all things consist.

Don't forget we're talking about the "Word" of God, now called Jesus, by whom all things were made and all things do consist. It's the Word…on this or that, that will produce….this or that!!

God makes things out of substance that already exists, like when He made Adam out of the dust of the ground and then Eve out of Adam's rib. God also creates things out of nothing. But wait!! God uses Words…to create.

We can now see that the substance…is in the words themselves. All the generic information in the word RED, will produce the color red. What do you want in life? God has given us the ability to use words, and the Word Himself…Jesus said, "Whatsoever you shall ask in My name….I WILL DO IT!!" What do you want? A car, a house, a husband or wife? Frame it with words, like God framed the creation and restoration in Genesis.

Heb. 11:1
Now faith is the substance of things hoped for, the evidence of things not seen.

There are things that accompany Righteousness. And the right to call things that be not as though they were, is one of them. What do you want in life? Frame it with words, believe you receive it when you are "framing," as a done deal. Your words will take root, produce a plant, and the plant will produce the fruit thereof. Every seed will produce after it's own kind.

Come on think!! Hear with your heart, not your head.

Lk. 12:32
Fear not, little flock; for it is your Father's good pleasure to give you the kingdom.

●●●

Day - 3
"The Double Minded Man"
(James 1:1-8)

Kingdom Seekers
WEEK 11 DAY 3
02-26-2014

Jas. 1:1-8
1. James, a servant of God and of the Lord Jesus Christ, to the twelve tribes which are scattered abroad, greeting.
2. My brethren, count it all joy when ye fall into divers temptations;
3. Knowing this, that the trying of your faith worketh patience.
4. But let patience have her perfect work, that ye may be perfect and entire, wanting nothing.
5. If any of you lack wisdom, let him ask of God, that giveth to all men liberally, and upbraideth not; and it shall be given him.
6. But let him ask in faith, nothing wavering. For he that wavereth is like a wave of the sea driven with the wind and tossed.
7. For let not that man think that he shall receive any thing of the Lord.
8. A double minded man is unstable in all his ways.

Have you asked God for something and then set about to do the doing of it yourself? Here in America, we are taught to man up, take care of things ourselves, men don't cry, and deal with it!! It's a natural tendency to try to take care of business ourselves, and not lean on anyone else.

I'm not trying to find fault here. I just want to point out that if you have asked your Father God for something, let God be God. Every good and perfect gift comes down from above.

You could very accurately describe The KINGDOM of GOD, as a backwards Kingdom. In order to live, one must first die. In order to be exalted, one must first humble himself. In order to receive, one must first give.

I'll give an example in my own life. I asked God for a new truck. Instead of saving money for the truck, I started sowing money into several TV ministries, and a local church. Why? Because I had asked for the truck to come paid for.

Using the laws and principles I had learned about The KINGDOM of GOD, I learned not to save for the truck, but to sow seed…for the truck. Every seed produces after it's own kind. Money is not the only seed available to us. We can sow time, clothing, food, money, love, the possibilities are endless. If you want a small ranch and you have a city lot somewhere, sow it to the city, or a family that needs it or a ministry that might need some land. I got my truck and it came paid for, praise God!!

The point is, if you ask God for something, don't try to do it for yourself. Literally, I received the truck that night when I asked God for it. When the time came for the manifestation, the money was there waiting for me, in other words, the money was not out of pocket. God provided both the truck AND the money to buy it with too.

There is much to be learned about The KINGDOM of GOD. Everything has it's purpose, has it's place, has it's principle. Believe me, once we learn how the system works, we can work the system at will. The Word will work everytime we put it to work, but as Paul told Timothy,

2 Tim. 2:5-7
5. And if a man also strive for masteries, yet is he not crowned, except he strive lawfully.
6. The husbandman that laboureth must be first partaker of the fruits.
7. Consider what I say; and the Lord give thee understanding in all things.

In other words, do it according to knowledge, not speculation, just asking God for something and then hoping that you get it, is NOT proper procedure. Ask, believing that you receive it even as you are asking, without money, and without price, it'll come if you faint not. Hold fast to your confession of faith.

Heb. 10:23
Let us hold fast the profession of our faith without wavering; (for he is faithful that promised;

Heb. 12:2
Looking unto Jesus the author and finisher of our faith.

The Author: The Bible, and God's promises…

The Finisher: By Jesus working with us confirming the Word with signs following.

If you have something you want to do, I don't think God has a problem with that, knock yourself out, but if you ask God to do something for you…don't touch it again in your thought life, or even one of your fingers. Let God, be God.

Mt. 18:3
And said, Verily I say unto you, Except ye be converted, and become as little children, ye shall not enter into the kingdom of heaven.

Except ye be converted…. That's referring to the renewing of the mind, have you done that?

*Become as little children…*that's believing and putting Faith in the Word of God.

Not enter into the Kingdom… I think Jesus means, not enter into the "knowledge" of The KINGDOM, whereby we can live out our lives according to KINGDOM RULE on the earth.

Mk. 10:25
It is easier for a camel to go through the eye of a needle, than for a rich man to enter into the kingdom of God.

A self willed man. If God doesn't take care of this in my timing, I'll take care of it myself.

Double minded!!

Lk. 12:32
Fear not, little flock; for it is your Father's good pleasure to give you the kingdom.

●●●●

Day - 4
"Ambassadors For Christ"
(II Corinthians 5:20)

Kingdom Seekers
WEEK 11 DAY 4
02-27-2014

2 Co.5:20-21
20. Now then we are ambassadors for Christ, as though God did beseech you by us: we pray you in Christ's stead, be ye reconciled to God.
21. For he hath made him to be sin for us, who knew no sin; that we might be made the righteousness of God in him.

What is the primary interest of an ambassador? To establish equitable relations with other persons, companies, entities, or countries.

We call it the great commission or the ministry of reconciliation. God working with us to save souls to eternal life. Why is God working with us? Because heaven is God's domain, the earth is our domain. Anything God does on the earth is because we ask God to intervene on our behalf.

God has given us free will. That's why crime runs so rampant in the world today. It's the sin nature of the flesh. That's why we are told to renew our minds.

Ro. 12:2

And be not conformed to this world: but be ye transformed by the renewing of your mind, that ye may prove what is that good, and acceptable, and perfect, will of God.

Did you notice that God is not responsible for proving His will on the earth, WE are.

Eph. 3:10
To the intent that now unto the principalities and powers in heavenly places might be known by the church the manifold wisdom of God,

...might be known by the church the manifold wisdom of God. That's us!!

Mt. 16:19
And I will give unto thee the keys of the kingdom of heaven: and whatsoever thou shalt bind on earth shall be bound in heaven: and whatsoever thou shalt loose on earth shall be loosed in heaven.

An Ambassador never gives his or her own personal opinion. They always state the policy of their country. Thank God for all His promises. They are God's will for His people, the answers for all our needs.

1 Jo. 5:13-15
13. These things have I written unto you that believe on the name of the Son of God; that ye may know that ye have eternal life, and that ye may believe on the name of the Son of God.
14. And this is the confidence that we have in him, that, if we ask any thing according to his will, he heareth us:
15. And if we know that he hear us, whatsoever we ask, we know that we have the petitions that we desired of him.

I've used this illustration before but it bares repeating. Israel, is described in the Bible as God's jewel. When light hits a jewel, the light shoots out like a lighthouse by the sea.

The Church, on the other hand, is described as a pearl of great price. A pearl doesn't shoot out a beam of light, it absorbs light. The church is more like a street light.

They say that the natural eye can see the light from a candle flame from several miles away. I don't know about that, but I do know that we can see a street light from MANY miles away.

We are being watched. You never hear of a person exclaiming, I can't believe they did that!! After all....they're Buddhists!!! Or they're Hindus, or some other religion, No, no, people are surprised because it was a Christian that did it. That tells me that the world knows what godliness should be like. We are the standard, we are the comparison by which God, and godliness, is judged on the earth.

Mt. 5:13-16

13. Ye are the salt of the earth: but if the salt have lost his savour, wherewith shall it be salted? it is thenceforth good for nothing, but to be cast out, and to be trodden under foot of men.

14. Ye are the light of the world. A city that is set on an hill cannot be hid.

15. Neither do men light a candle, and put it under a bushel, but on a candlestick; and it giveth light unto all that are in the house.

16. Let your light so shine before men, that they may see your good works, and glorify your Father which is in heaven.

If you haven't renewed your mind, you have a long way to go Bubba, and YOU know it. If you are still subject to sickness and disease and financial distress, it's simply because you don't know who you are in Christ. The curse of the law is still out there.

1 Pet. 5:6-10
6. Humble yourselves therefore under the mighty hand of God, that he may exalt you in due time:
7. Casting all your care upon him; for he careth for you.
8. Be sober, be vigilant; because your adversary the devil, as a roaring lion, walketh about, seeking whom he may devour:
9. Whom resist stedfast in the faith, knowing that the same afflictions are accomplished in your brethren that are in the world.
10. But the God of all grace, who hath called us unto his eternal glory by Christ Jesus, after that ye have suffered a while, make you perfect, stablish, strengthen, settle you.

(v.9) reminds me of verse 3 in Gal. 4. *Even so we, when we were children, were in bondage under the elements of the world:*

Until we grow up in Christ, we are still in bondage to the elements, and the same afflictions that are in the world. BUT, as we learn who we are in Christ, we can learn how to stand against these things and overcome them. That's what Father God wants the world to see…that we are living a blessed life able to overcome whatever comes against us by using the Word.

If you have just started following this Bible study, you need to go back to the beginning, Week-1-Day-1. We are now in Week-11-Day-4. Every lesson is built on the previous lesson and or lessons. For instance, when I just said, "by using the Word." you need to go back to Weel-2-Days 2, 3, 4, and 5, Week-3-Days 1, 2, and 3, Week-4-Days 1-5. Week-5-Days 1-5. If you don't know or understand what is being said today, it's because you don't know what was said yesterday. This study is progressive. It is built on a solid foundation of The Word of God,

Lk. 12:32
Fear not, little flock; for it is your Father's good pleasure to give you the kingdom.

● ● ● ● ●

Day - 5
"Entering God's Rest II"
(Hebrews 3:10 and 4:16)

Kingdom Seekers
WEEK 11 DAY 5
02-28-2014

Heb. 3:8-11
8. Harden not your hearts, as in the provocation, in the day of temptation in the wilderness:
9. When your fathers tempted me, proved me, and saw my works forty years.
10. Wherefore I was grieved with that generation, and said, They do alway err in their heart; and they have not known my ways.
11. So I sware in my wrath, They shall not enter into my rest.

I know we covered this before but I want to re-iterate. Working along day by day and waiting for Saturday to get our answers from God is not what I'm seeing here in Heb. 3. The Bible doesn't teach that, but the Bible does teach that we are to work all week, then rest on Saturday.

So what's Heb. 3 saying to us?
● 1 They have not known my ways.
● 2. They shall not enter into my rest.

Let's go back to Genesis 1:1-31. God said, and it was so. God said, and it was so. God said, and it was so!! And God saw that it was good.

We also included
Heb. 4:12
For the word of God is quick, and powerful, and sharper than any twoedged sword, piercing even to the dividing asunder of soul and spirit, and of the joints and marrow, and is a discerner of the thoughts and intents of the heart.

For the word of God is quick, and powerful, and is a discerner of the thoughts and intents of the heart.

Don't forget, we are talking about the Word of God, right now…not Jesus. Jesus was the "Word," long before He was Jesus. In the OT we have The Father, The Word, and The Spirit. In the NT we have The Father, The Son, And The Holy Ghost. We're talking about "The Word" right now, not "The Son."

At this point, let me bring up

Heb. 6:1

Therefore leaving the principles of the doctrine of Christ, let us go on unto perfection; not laying again the foundation of repentance from dead works, and of faith toward God.

I have been trying to get you to make the distinction between Jesus, and who Jesus was, before He was Jesus, for some time now. Jesus is, was, and always will be "The Word of God!!"

Now…let's see what was going on in Genesis. When God said, Let there be Light!! The Word of God, which was in God, went out and created the sun.

Jo. 1:1-3

1. In the beginning was the Word, and the Word was with God, and the Word was God.

2. The same was in the beginning with God.

3. All things were made by him; and without him …(The Word)… was not any thing made that was made.

So we see that when God speaks, "The Word," which is in God, goes out and performs the doing…of what God said!! When we see that God saw that it was good, we can deduce that the Word that was in God, knew what God was thinking when God said it and, the Word knew what God had intended, when God said that. Right? God put the Word out there, entered into rest on the deal, "expecting" until His Words came to pass. Does that sound kosher to you? Can we say that? I believe that's what Heb. 3:8-11 is implying…not working for 5 days and resting on Saturday.

My point is this. The Word that was in God in Genesis…now lives in you!

The Word…now called Jesus said in

Jo. 14:10-14

10. Believest thou not that I am in the Father, and the Father in me? the words that I speak unto you I speak not of myself: but the Father that dwelleth in me, he doeth the works.

11. Believe me that I am in the Father, and the Father in me: or else believe me for the very works' sake.

12. Verily, verily, I say unto you, He that believeth on me, the works that I do shall he do also; and greater works than these shall he do; because I go unto my Father.

13. And whatsoever ye shall ask in my name, that will I do, that the Father may be glorified in the Son.

14. If ye shall ask any thing in my name, I will do it.

Jesus…The Word, just told you that He does everything that God says, and now…He will do everything that we ask in His Name!! How cool is that? Of course what we ask for needs to line up with Bible truth, and the promises that are recorded in the Bible, and spoken in righteousness and true holiness.

The KINGDOM of GOD is an agrarian society. We don't have money, or tools, or an abundance of supplies. All we have in The KINGDOM of GOD, at our disposal are Words. Words… are the rate of exchange in The KINGDOM, the ONLY rate of exchange available to us and it is outrageous in its buying power, and dynamic in its working. We can buy a tooth brush, or a multi-million dollar office complex with "Words." We can change a diseased heart into a brand new heart simply by using "Words." All the riches we will ever need, we already have….in abundance….a never ending supply.

What do you want in life? Speak it, frame it with "Words" just like God did in Genesis. The "Word," as a seed, will produce what you say….if you can believe…for it to work for you. Don't worry about a thing, as you grow in Christ, you will be persuaded to believe. You go ahead and put your word out there, enter into the "God kind of rest," and as we would say today, just hide and watch, just see if your words come to pass….or not.

Lk. 12:32
Fear not, little flock; for it is your Father's good pleasure to give you the kingdom.

■ ▢ ■ ▢ ■ ▢ ■ ▢ ■ ▢ ■ ▢

Week-12
The Power of His Resurrection

Week-12-Days-1-5
The Whole Armour of God:
Day-1. The Armour of God. Eph. 6:10-17
Day-2. Casting Down Imaginations. 2 Co. 10:3-6
Day-3. Water Baptism. Jo. 3:5 & Mt. 3:13-15
Day-4. Principalities and Powers. Eph. 6:12
Day-5. Whatsoever Ye Shall Ask in My Name, I WILL DO IT!! Jo. 14:13-14

●

Day - 1
"The Armour of God"
(Ephesians 6:10-17)

Kingdom Seekers
WEEK 12 DAY 1
03-03-2014

Eph. 6:10-17
10. Finally, my brethren, be strong in the Lord, and in the power of his might.
11. Put on the whole armour of God, that ye may be able to stand against the wiles of the devil.
12. For we wrestle not against flesh and blood, but against principalities, against powers, against the rulers of the darkness of this world, against spiritual wickedness in high places.
13. Wherefore take unto you the whole armour of God, that ye may be able to withstand in the evil day, and having done all, to stand.
14. Stand therefore, having your loins girt about with truth, and having on the breastplate of righteousness;
15. And your feet shod with the preparation of the gospel of peace;
16. Above all, taking the shield of faith, wherewith ye shall be able to quench all the fiery darts of the wicked.
17. And take the helmet of salvation, and the sword of the Spirit, which is the word of God:

We will be talking about principalities and powers on Day-4 this week. For now I want us to focus on "having done all to stand." The Lord has taken us through a lot of material in this Bible study. A lot of truth. Though we don't know it all, I believe we have come a long way in learning how to live life in The KINGDOM of GOD. The armour we will be looking at is designed to advance and take ground, not to retreat to a former position. By that I mean, there is no armour on our back, God, is described as our rear reward….God is our protection and our guarantee, He watches over His Word, to perform it. How does He do that? By confirming His Word with signs following, God has got our back!!

Mk. 16:20
And they went forth, and preached every where, the Lord working with them, and confirming the word with signs following. Amen.

Heb. 2:4
God also bearing them witness, both with signs and wonders, and with divers miracles, and gifts of the Holy Ghost, according to his own will.

We have seen that we don't have to call Jesus in on the scene to deliver us from our circumstances, the Word, is nigh us, even in our mouth and in our heart, that is the Word of Faith, which we preach. The disciple is not above his Master, it is enough that the disciple be AS his Master. When we have a problem, WE are to take care of it using the Word of Truth to deliver us from our circumstances, having your loins girt about with truth, (knowing our authority and the power we have in Christ). and having on the breastplate of righteousness; again, (knowing who we are in Christ). And your feet shod with the preparation of the gospel of peace; (is this the gospel of salvation, or the gospel of The KINGDOM? I believe it is not salvation, but KINGDOM gospel! You choose!!

Jesus said, with what measure you meet, it will be measured unto you. It is also written, From Faith to Faith, as it is written, the just shall live by Faith. From Faith unto salvation, to Faith in the Word, as a way of life in The KINGDOM.

1 Jo. 5:13
These things have I written unto you that believe on the name of the Son of God; that ye may know that ye have eternal life, and that ye may believe on the name of the Son of God.

Two different believings here. One to salvation and the knowledge that we have eternal life, and the other, unto believing God's Word, and living out our lives according to the promises recorded in the Word of God, in The KINGDOM of GOD!!

Above all, taking the shield of faith, wherewith ye shall be able to quench all the fiery darts of the wicked.

Our will is involved here. Are you believing for the promises to protect you…or not? If you're believing…. that's Faith!! That's the shield of Faith that will protect you in times of trouble. And take the helmet of salvation... That's peace of mind in the knowledge of eternal life and the assurance of the Word of God, working in our lives.

Mt. 11:28-30

28. Come unto me, all ye that labour and are heavy laden, and I will give you rest.

29. Take my yoke upon you, and learn of me; for I am meek and lowly in heart: and ye shall find rest unto your souls.

30. For my yoke is easy, and my burden is light.

Put your trust in the Word...Jesus. Jesus has the answers to all our needs, the author and finisher, of our Faith!!

...and the sword of the Spirit, which is the word of God:

Find a promise that covers your need, speak it, doubt not in your heart, but believe that what you said shall come to pass. Jesus said, that if any one would do that, he shall have what he said!!!

Jesus also said,

Mk. 4:21-25

21. And he said unto them, Is a candle brought to be put under a bushel, or under a bed? and not to be set on a candlestick?

22. For there is nothing hid, which shall not be manifested; neither was any thing kept secret, but that it should come abroad.

23. If any man have ears to hear, let him hear.

24. And he said unto them, Take heed what ye hear: with what measure ye mete, it shall be measured to you: and unto you that hear shall more be given.

25. For he that hath, to him shall be given: and he that hath not, from him shall be taken even that which he hath.

Lk. 12:32

Fear not, little flock; for it is your Father's good pleasure to give you the kingdom.

●●

Day - 2
"Casting Down Imaginations"
(2 Corinthians 10:3-6)

Kingdom Seekers
WEEK 12 DAY 2
03-04-2014

2 Co. 10:3-6

3. For though we walk in the flesh, we do not war after the flesh:

4. (For the weapons of our warfare are not carnal, but mighty through God to the pulling down of strong holds;)

    5. Casting down imaginations, and every high thing that exalteth itself against the knowledge of God, and bringing into captivity every thought to the obedience of Christ;

    6. And having in a readiness to revenge all disobedience, when your obedience is fulfilled.

…For though we walk in the flesh, we do not war after the flesh…

We don't go to court….we don't seek an injunction…we don't fight city hall with a picket line. When we fight or otherwise, take a stand, it's against principalities and powers, and rulers of darkness in high places. We'll talk about this issue in Week-12-Day-4. What we're going to see now is the fact that we have the God given right to take a legal, spiritual, stand against anything that doesn't line up with the knowledge of God.

…Casting down imaginations, and every high thing that exalteth itself against the knowledge of God…

God's knowledge is exact knowledge!!

Psa. 103:3
Who forgiveth all thine iniquities; who healeth all thy diseases…

Mt. 8:17b
Himself took our infirmities, and bare our sicknesses…

1 Pet. 2:24b
…by whose stripes ye were healed.

There is no gray area in these scriptures. They mean exactly what they say. So, why are we still sick????

We have yet to cast down imaginations and every high thing that exalts itself against the KNOWLEDGE of God. There are people who still think that God made them sick, to teach them something. How stupid is that, in view of what we see in scripture?

I have a handout I use in class with 135 healing scriptures on it. Anyone of them can produce healing. I tell the class to pick one that you are comfortable with, speak it, doubt not in your heart, but believe that it can effect a healing for you. I say that because Jesus said, for anyone that would do that, he shall have what he said! Right?

…and bringing into captivity every thought to the obedience of Christ… (or, The Word.)

That comes under the heading of renewing the mind… from the thoughts and ways of the world…to the thoughts and ways of God…in GOD'S KINGDOM. You are healed right now. As soon as you can agree with that and accept it…your manifestation should take place.

Psa. 23:5a
Thou preparest a table before me in the presence of mine enemies…

sickness and disease are enemies….divine health… is on the table!!

…And having in a readiness to revenge all disobedience…

Stop speculating, guessing, surmising. The Word of God is clear. No sickness or disease has power over you. You have authority over all sickness and disease, CAST THEM OUT IN THE NAME OF JESUS period…paragraph!!!

…when your obedience is fulfilled…

After having done all to stand…stand therefore.

Hold fast, your confession. Don't quit and don't give up. The manifestation is coming. Jesus will confirm the Word with signs following, if you faint not.

Heb. 6:12
That ye be not slothful, but followers of them who through faith and patience inherit the promises.

It's all so simple when you know how the system works. It all revolves around "words." Faith filled Words…contain the power of The KINGDOM. The power to produce the promise, is in the promise itself. God doesn't have to lift a finger, the promise, like a seed, will produce what it describes or says. Simple…even child's play, when we see it for what it is.

The Bible is our measuring stick. If what's going on out there lines up with the Word, we should accept it as a blessing. If what's going on out there does not line up with the Word, we should reject it with power and might.

Let me encourage you, if you have just started this Bible study, go back to the beginning, Week-1-Day-1. This study will change everything for you. If you knew that you could stand against the wiles of the devil, I know you would….I just know you would!! The only weapon we have, is the only weapon we need…the Word of God!!

All the rest of the armour is protective gear. Preparation gear…Knowledge gear. Be a doer of the Word, not a hearer only, deceiving your own selves. You are in charge. Dictate policy in your own life. What do you want? Frame it with words, doubt not in your heart, but believe it will come to pass in your life. Others can learn from you.

Lk. 12:32
Fear not, little flock; for it is your Father's good pleasure to give you the kingdom.

●●●

Day - 3
"Water Baptism"
(John 3:5 and Matthew 3:13-15)

Kingdom Seekers
WEEK 12 DAY 3
03-05-2014

Jo. 3:3
Verily, verily, I say unto thee, Except a man be born again, he cannot see the kingdom of God.

The KINGDOM, in a very real way, is a mystery hidden in God. Much like salvation was a mystery, but now we are blasting it out all over the world. The KINGDOM however, is still a mystery to the natural man. Even the born again man. It is the spirit that quickens, the flesh profits nothing. The natural man, the carnal mind of reason, cannot look into, perceive, understand, neither can it know the things of God, for they are foolishness unto him.

1 Co. 2:14
But the natural man receiveth not the things of the Spirit of God: for they are foolishness unto him: neither can he know them, because they are spiritually discerned.

1 Co. 2:9-13
9. But as it is written, Eye hath not seen, nor ear heard, neither have entered into the heart of man, the things which God hath prepared for them that love him.
10. But God hath revealed them unto us by his Spirit: for the Spirit searcheth all things, yea, the deep things of God.
11. For what man knoweth the things of a man, save the spirit of man which is in him? even so the things of God knoweth no man, but the Spirit of God.
12. Now we have received, not the spirit of the world, but the spirit which is of God; that we might know the things that are freely given to us of God.
13. Which things also we speak, not in the words which man's wisdom teacheth, but which the Holy Ghost teacheth; comparing spiritual things with spiritual.

One of the things that the Holy Spirit does is to guide us into all truth.

Jesus said in *Jo. 8:31-32*
31. If ye continue in my word, then are ye my disciples indeed;

32. And ye shall know the truth, and the truth shall make you free.

Let's consider the truth of Water Baptism. let the natural eye see what it sees, and the Spiritual eye see what it sees.

Jo. 3:5
Verily, verily, I say unto thee, Except a man be born of water and of the Spirit, he cannot enter into the kingdom of God.

Okay, this could be being born of natural childbirth. "her water broke" type water, or it could mean born of being anointed by holy water, or it could mean being born of the washing of the water of the Word, or even something else.

So I looked up the Greek word for water. It is #5204 in Strong's concordance. The word is hudor (hoo-dore) it means water (as if rainy) water. Just common ordinary water, type water. So we're talking about rain water, river water, sea water, ocean water, natural, "not supernatural," water.

Mt. 3:13-15
13. Then cometh Jesus from Galilee to Jordan unto John, to be baptized of him.
14. But John forbad him, saying, I have need to be baptized of thee, and comest thou to me?
15. And Jesus answering said unto him, Suffer it to be so now: for thus it becometh us to fulfil all righteousness. Then he suffered him.

The Bible teaches the baptism of John unto repentance. The Bible also teaches the baptism of John for the forgiveness of sins. The question is, what is God's purpose for water baptism? We have seen man's interpretation of water baptism, now let's see what God has to say about it!! We see it in verse 15. It is to fulfill all Righteousness!! No other reason. The word "becometh" I don't know why I looked it up but I'm glad I did.

It is the Greek word, 'prepo' [#4241] *(prep-o)* it means; to tower up (be conspicuous), to be suitable or proper, fit or right, become, comely.

Consider this, if Jesus thought it was important to be baptized, we too should think it important to be baptized.

A key phrase taken from
Act. 1:22
Beginning from the baptism of John, unto that same day that he was taken up from us, must one be ordained to be a witness with us of his resurrection.

Beginning from the baptism of John, unto that same day that he was taken up from us...

That statement can be said of our forerunners in Christ, as well. EW Kenyon, John G. Lake,

Smith Wigglesworth, Kenneth Hagen, Billy Jo Dougherty, and so on.

Beginning from the baptism of John, unto that same day that he or she was taken up from us…

There's more to being baptized than meet the eye. We don't need to be baptized to repent. We repented when we asked Jesus to come into our hearts and save us. We don't need to be baptized for the forgiveness of sins. We were forgiven when Jesus came into our hearts and saved us. Jesus didn't need to repent, or have His sins forgiven, He was baptized in order to "fulfill all righteousness," right? Also, I believe Jesus was identifying with His own death, burial, &resurrection.

Ro. 6:3-5
3. Know ye not, that so many of us as were baptized into Jesus Christ were baptized into his death?
4. Therefore we are buried with him by baptism into death: that like as Christ was raised up from the dead by the glory of the Father, even so we also should walk in newness of life.
5. For if we have been planted together in the likeness of his death, we shall be also in the likeness of his resurrection:

Jesus submitted to water baptism for two reasons.
▶ 1. To fulfill all righteousness.
▶ 2. To personally identify with His own death, burial, and resurrection.

When we do it, we do the same!!

• NOTES •
Water Baptism

Ro. 6:3-5
3. Know ye not, that so many of us as were baptized into Jesus Christ were baptized into his death?
4. Therefore we are buried with him by baptism into death: that like as Christ was raised up from the dead by the glory of the Father, even so we also should walk in newness of life.
5. For if we have been planted together in the likeness of his death, we shall be also in the likeness of his resurrection:

When we are baptized, we, like Jesus, fulfill all righteousness, AND personally identify with Jesus' death, burial, and resurrection…. and *(v.5) For if we have been planted together in the likeness of his death, we shall be also in the likeness of his resurrection:*

Jesus did no ministry, no work, no miracle until after He was baptized. The most one could say He did was to read from the scriptures from time to time in the Synagogue. Other than that, he was not involved in ministry.

In Jo. 1:1-36 is the account of Jesus being baptized with John's baptism…. water baptism

Then we have in

Jo. 2:11

This beginning of miracles did Jesus in Cana of Galilee, and manifested forth his glory; and his disciples believed on him.

Jesus started His ministry after the baptism of John....water baptism.

1 Co. 10:1-4

1. Moreover, brethren, I would not that ye should be ignorant, how that all our fathers were under the cloud, and all passed through the sea;

2. And were all baptized unto Moses in the cloud and in the sea;

3. And did all eat the same spiritual meat;

4. And did all drink the same spiritual drink: for they drank of that spiritual Rock that followed them: and that Rock was Christ.

Moses' baptism? What? Like I said before, there is more to baptism than meets the eye...that is to say... the natural eye, that leads to the natural mind of reason. How many times in the sermon on the mount did Jesus say, You have heard it said, but I say? You have heard it said, but I say!!

Water baptism in the OT was indeed for repentance and for the forgiveness of sins. That was an OT truth. Why? Because after baptism in the sea, the gospel was preached. They had fulfilled all righteousness, and now they could "hear" the gospel...and do it!! That... was the significance of water baptism in the Old Testament. It was done so that they could hear and do the gospel. Now in the New Testament we have a new significance for water baptism. It is a starting point for our own ministry. Just as it was for Jesus. A new beginning, a newness of life. Paul said it this way, "O to know Him and the power of His resurrection."

Isa. 35:1-10. Read it all.

This is verse 8.

And an highway shall be there, and a way, and it shall be called The way of holiness; the unclean shall not pass over it; but it shall be for those: the wayfaring men, though fools, shall not err therein.

Go ahead and read all of Isa.35. It's only 10 verses.

The Way of Holiness. Wow. Only the redeemed shall walk there...the ransomed of the Lord. That's us!!

I looked up the word Highway. It is #4547 macluwl *(mas-lool)* a thoroughfare (as turnpiked) highway.

Well hey, this is Oklahoma, we know turnpikes. There are some things we know about turnpikes. They are privately owned, privately built, and maintained. They are a straight shot from point A. to point B. AND there is a toll gate. We can't pay our way through this toll gate. We can't earn our way through it either. Could it be that water baptism is our ticket through the toll gate?

A kind of "right of passage?"

I didn't put this 'Notes on Water Baptism' in the official Bible study because I can't prove what I'm saying. I told you earlier, I sometimes teach things that the Bible doesn't flat out say, or teach. Thank God, you don't have to believe this in order to be saved. Are we indeed...on The Way of Holiness? It is a Highway, and a Way. John prepared "the way" of the Lord.

Isa. 40:3-4
3. The voice of him that crieth in the wilderness, Prepare ye the way of the LORD, make straight in the desert a highway for our God.
4. Every valley shall be exalted, and every mountain and hill shall be made low: and the crooked shall be made straight, and the rough places plain:

...speak the Word only, and my servant will be healed...a statement of strong Faith!! That's how things are done in The KINGDOM of GOD. Speaking Words...it's Words only... in The KINGDOM of GOD. We don't have to go to the temple to pray. We don't have to bring the sick to Jerusalem. The "Way" has been made. The road that John built, the way of holiness, the way of the Lord!!

Some, will spit this teaching up, but retain it. Others will spit this teaching out and forget it. Like I said, you don't have to believe this in order to be saved.

For those who receive this teaching, it may enhance the impact of your ministry, giving you more confidence than you may have had before. Let the Spirit which is within you bare witness whether this be of a truth, or not.

It is your Father's good pleasure to give you The KINGDOM.

●●●●

Day - 4
"Principalities and Powers"
(Ephesians 6:12)

Kingdom Seekers
WEEK 12 DAY 4
03-06-2014

Eph. 6:9-12
9. And, ye masters, do the same things unto them, forbearing threatening: knowing that your Master also is in heaven; neither is there respect of persons with him.
10. Finally, my brethren, be strong in the Lord, and in the power of his might.
11. Put on the whole armour of God, that ye may be able to stand against the wiles of the devil.
12. For we wrestle not against flesh and blood, but against principalities, against powers, against the rulers of the darkness of this world, against spiritual wickedness in high places.

Our fight is not with the school board, or the police department, or the local city , or state government. Our fight is with principalities, and powers. Rulers of darkness in high places. Our weapons are not knives and guns, but the Word of God, or in other words, like we've been saying all along in this Bible study, Words…God's Words, in the form of the promises, and our own words. Jesus will do them all.

Jo. 14:13-14
13. And whatsoever ye shall ask in my name, that will I do, that the Father may be glorified in the Son.
14. If ye shall ask any thing in my name, I will do it.

It's His job! It's what He does! Jesus fulfills, and brings to pass…Words!!

The Bible puts it this way,
Mk. 16:20
And they went forth, and preached every where, the Lord working with them, and confirming the word with signs following. Amen.

Jesus confirms words… with signs following. If we can only get in line with this truth, Jesus will confirm OUR words with signs following. It is principalities and powers that are coming against us, not people. Rulers of darkness aligned with them to defeat us, demoralize us, to ultimately kill us. Misery loves company. Only this is more than misery, it is vengeance!! They know their end, and they're not willing to go to their place alone.

Jesus died for the whole world, not just those of us who believe. That means, there are forgiven men and women going to hell because they have rejected that forgiveness, because that forgiveness comes in the person of Jesus, of Nazareth, the man, the Christ!! The enemy has blinded their minds of the redemption that is in Christ. All we have to fight this fight with, is the Word of God, the sword of the Spirit.

Heb. 4:12
For the word of God is quick, and powerful, and sharper than any twoedged sword, piercing even to the dividing asunder of soul and spirit, and of the joints and marrow, and is a discerner of the thoughts and intents of the heart.

When and as we minister, the Word that is in us knows what we are thinking and what we intend, as we speak. As we minister, we don't have to be as articulate as most preachers say. The Word is in us, He knows what you're thinking. You don't have to be so meticulous in your description of what you want, He knows what color and how many, or whatever...he knows!! Just speak the Word only...He's got your back.

Don't forget, there is a time frame to receive the results, in The KINGDOM of GOD.

Mk. 4:26-29
26. And he said, So is the kingdom of God, as if a man should cast seed into the ground;
27. And should sleep, and rise night and day, and the seed should spring and grow up, he knoweth not how.
28. For the earth bringeth forth fruit of herself; first the blade, then the ear, after that the full corn in the ear.
29. But when the fruit is brought forth, immediately he putteth in the sickle, because the harvest is come.

This is probably where most all of us fail...The Time Frame!! This is America!! We want it NOW!! And we are used to having it now!!

Jas. 1:3-4
3. Knowing this, that the trying of your faith worketh patience.
4. But let patience have her perfect work, that ye may be perfect and entire, wanting nothing.

You are in charge!! You dictate policy in your own life. When you minister into the lives of others, you help them through your Faith, to dictate policy in their lives. You know...Jesus ministered by his own Faith for who knows how long, but the day came, when he said, daughter, YOUR Faith hath made you whole.

Can others be delivered by YOUR Faith? Sure, we are Ambassadors for Christ on the earth, aren't we? Don't lose your ability to think, just because you know you're a supernatural being. We are to grow to the stature of the fullness of Christ.

Mk. 16:15-18

15. Go ye into all the world, and preach the gospel to every creature.

16. He that believeth and is baptized shall be saved; but he that believeth not shall be damned.

17. And these signs shall follow them that believe; In my name shall they cast out devils; they shall speak with new tongues;

18. They shall take up serpents; and if they drink any deadly thing, it shall not hurt them; they shall lay hands on the sick, and they shall recover.

Jo. 14:12

Verily, verily, I say unto you, He that believeth on me, the works that I do shall he do also; and greater works than these shall he do; because I go unto my Father. It is your Father's good pleasure to give you the kingdom.

●●●●●

Day - 5
"Whatsoever Ye Shall Ask in My Name, I WILL DO IT!"
(John 14:13-14)

Kingdom Seekers
WEEK 12 DAY 5
03-07-2014

Jo. 14:10-14

10. Believest thou not that I am in the Father, and the Father in me? the words that I speak unto you I speak not of myself: but the Father that dwelleth in me, he doeth the works.

11. Believe me that I am in the Father, and the Father in me: or else believe me for the very works' sake.

12. Verily, verily, I say unto you, He that believeth on me, the works that I do shall he do also; and greater works than these shall he do; because I go unto my Father.

13. And whatsoever ye shall ask in my name, that will I do, that the Father may be glorified in the Son.

14. If ye shall ask any thing in my name, I will do it.

(See: Mk. 16:17) This passage is one of the principle teachings of the authority we have in Christ Jesus.

What a charge!! What an honor...in Jesus' Name. Ambassadors for Christ. Co-laborers with God. Born again men and women, under authority,

Mt. 16:19

And I will give unto thee the keys of the kingdom of heaven: and whatsoever thou shalt bind on

earth shall be bound in heaven: and whatsoever thou shalt loose on earth shall be loosed in heaven.

Mt. 17:20b
...If ye have faith as a grain of mustard seed, ye shall say unto this mountain, Remove hence to yonder place; and it shall remove; and nothing shall be impossible unto you.

All things are possible to us. It doesn't matter if it costs a lot of money or takes a lot of tools or equipment. All we need is the right words, to do the job.

Jo. 15:7
If ye abide in me, and my words abide in you, ye shall ask what ye will, and it shall be done unto you.

If you believe that, you will be great, in The KINGDOM. If you don't believe it, you'll live out your life like the heathen, without hope, and without God's influence in your life. You are saved, but you will be on your own. There are too many of us that insist on "I did it my way," and not trust in God's way. The Word, is the Way.

Ro. 8:6
For to be carnally minded is death; but to be spiritually minded is life and peace.

A somewhat passive Faith statement, but effective,
Mt. 17:27
Notwithstanding, lest we should offend them, go thou to the sea, and cast an hook, and take up the fish that first cometh up; and when thou hast opened his mouth, thou shalt find a piece of money: that take, and give unto them for me and thee.

Okay, can you learn from this? Maybe, maybe not!! It's your choice. Will you be great in The KINGDOM?

Mt. 18:19-20
19. Again I say unto you, That if two of you shall agree on earth as touching any thing that they shall ask, it shall be done for them of my Father which is in heaven.
20. For where two or three are gathered together in my name, there am I in the midst of them.

Is Jesus there to glory in the fact that two agreed on something, or is He there to carry out the agreement? Again, you chose!!

(v.20) For where two or three are gathered together in my name, there am I in the midst of them.

When we agree on scripture, that brings Jesus in on the scene. You know that Jesus is going to agree, Jesus IS scripture!! Jesus will confirm the agreement with signs following, IF you agree, and believe for, whatever the agreement was for. Got it?

Jo. 14:21
He that hath my commandments, and keepeth them, he it is that loveth me: and he that loveth me shall be loved of my Father, and I will love him, and will manifest myself to him.

How will Jesus manifest Himself to us? By confirming His self with signs following. HEY, Jesus is the WORD!! Generally speaking, Jesus is not going to personally meet up with you in a personal visitation, but He will confirm himself by signs following.

Jo. 16:24
Hitherto have ye asked nothing in my name: ask, and ye shall receive, that your joy may be full.

Lk. 11:9-10
9. And I say unto you, Ask, and it shall be given you; seek, and ye shall find; knock, and it shall be opened unto you.
10. For every one that asketh receiveth; and he that seeketh findeth; and to him that knocketh it shall be opened.

The only way to have great success is to take God at his Word, and do it!! Do what? The Word!! How do we do the Word? By believing, and acting on it!!

Jas. 1:22
But be ye doers of the word, and not hearers only, deceiving your own selves.

Heb. 12:27
And this word, Yet once more, signifieth the removing of those things that are shaken, as of things that are made, that those things which cannot be shaken may remain.

The Word of God stands firm, established forever. We will live forever by the Words that come from the mouth of God…and our own words, as Jesus said.

The thing is…we can start now. Learn to think the way God thinks, and do things, God's way.

Heb. 3:9-10
9. When your fathers tempted me, proved me, and saw my works forty years.
10. Wherefore I was grieved with that generation, and said, They do alway err in their heart; and they have not known my ways.

Jo. 14:14
If ye shall ask any thing in my name, I WILL DO IT!!

Check out these other Great Books from
BOLD TRUTH PUBLISHING

by Adrienne Gottlieb
• ISRAEL'S LEGITIMACY
Why We Should Protect Israel At All Cost

• The Replacement Theology LIE

-----

by Daryl Holloman
• The Adventures of Hezekiah Hare & Ernie Byrd
A Children's Bible Adventure

• Seemed Good to THE HOLY GHOST
Five Anointed Teachings by Brother Daryl

-----

by Steve Young
• SIX FEET DEEP
Burying Your Past with Forgiveness

-----

by Paul Howard
• THE FAITH WALK
Keys to walking in VICTORY!

-----

by Aaron Jones
• The Confessions of a Victorious Believer
Speaking GOD'S WORD into your life

• In the SECRET PLACE of THE MOST HIGH
God's Word for Supernatural Healing, Deliverance and Protection

• SOUND From HEAVEN
Praying in Tongues for a Victorious Life

See more Books and all of our products at
www.BoldTruthPublishing.com

www.ingramcontent.com/pod-product-compliance
Lightning Source LLC
LaVergne TN
LVHW081315060426
835509LV00015B/1523